BUILD A BETTER
BRIDGE

SOCIAL POLICY FOR THE 21ST CENTURY

LANCE HILLSINGER

Copyright © 2022 by Lance Hillsinger.

All rights reserved. No part of this publication may be reproduced, distributed, or transmitted in any form or by any means, including photocopying, recording, or other electronic or mechanical methods, without the prior written permission of the author, except in the case of brief quotations embodied in critical reviews and certain other noncommercial uses permitted by copyright law.

Printed in the United States of America.

Library of Congress Control Number: 2022930657

ISBN	Paperback	978-1-68536-248-5
	Hardback	978-1-68536-249-2
	eBook	978-1-68536-602-5

Westwood Books Publishing LLC
Atlanta Financial Center
3343 Peachtree Rd NE Ste 145-725
Atlanta, GA 30326

www.westwoodbookspublishing.com

PREFACE

For most of my adult life, I was employed as a child protective services (cps) social worker. As a cps social worker, I've seen the underside of American lives: the public housing projects, the seedy by-the-week motels, and the rundown trailer parks.

I began my career in child welfare in Los Angeles County, then continued in San Luis Obispo County. San Luis Obispo County is just north of Santa Barbara County. When my wife and I moved to San Luis Obispo, on the salaries of two civil servants, we could just afford to buy a home. Now, the median price of a home in San Luis Obispo County is over $700,000. In San Luis Obispo County, as in much of the nation, homeownership has become unaffordable for much of the middle-class. The lack of affordable housing, both for purchase or to rent, is a major social issue in America in the 21st century.

In both Los Angeles and San Luis Obispo counties, I frequently had reason to interview inmates at the county jail. In Los Angeles County, almost all inmates were African-American or Hispanic; there were very few white faces. In San Luis Obispo, reflecting the population of the county, it was mostly whites and Hispanics in jail. As in jails and prisons everywhere, men greatly outnumbered women. Addressing the racial and gender in incarceration rates and the underlying racial and gender inequities in education are also major social issues of the 21st century.

In San Luis Obispo County, child protective services was part of the larger Department of Social Services (DSS). Besides Department of Social Services, other commons terms for the "welfare department" are the Department of Public Social Services, the Department of Family Services, and the Office of Economic Development. By whatever name "the welfare department" is called, social welfare programs use taxpayers' money and, in the form of cash aid, food stamps, housing assistance, etc., redistribute taxpayers' money to the needy. As detailed in the following chapters, several ideas are proposed to make better use of tax dollars.

Social welfare programs that began with the War of Poverty have reduced the poverty rate, but social programs do not create wealth. Wealth is created through capitalism. It is capitalism that finances innovation and creates jobs. However, just as reforms are needed in welfare programs, reforms are needed in capitalism. Under the present system, the rich have become even richer. The divide between the "haves" and the "have nots" is deeper than it has ever been.

As neither liberal nor conservative thinking has a monopoly on good (or bad) ideas, the ideas proposed in the following chapters are not based on any particular ideology. Many of the ideas presented cost little or nothing to implement. Even those ideas that cost appreciable amounts of money would comprise only a small fraction of the federal budget and, in most cases, would pay for themselves over time. But whether or not a particular idea "pencils out," government has a moral obligation to the needy. Caring for those unable to fully support themselves is a fundamental moral obligation of good government.

While the government has a moral obligation to the poor, it also has a fiduciary obligation to the taxpayer. This fiduciary obligation means good stewardship of taxpayer's money. Good stewardship means taxpayer dollars are leveraged to the greatest extent possible. Government needs to work towards an America where homeless shelters and food banks are closing because not for lack of funding but because they are no longer needed.

Moreover, change in social policy is also needed to keep America competitive in the global economy. For America to hold its own in the economy of the 21st century, vigorous funding for research and infrastructure is required. However, government budgets are limited. A tax dollar spent for basic research or infrastructure is a tax dollar not spent for the needy and vice versa.

Finally, change is needed both in social welfare programs and in capitalism so that, as has been true in the past, each succeeding generation of Americans has a better standard of living than the previous.

STYLISTIC CONVENTIONS

The stylistic conventions of the APA (American Psychological Association) are used throughout the social sciences, not just in psychology. However, APA stylistic guidelines don't always give a full picture. For example, under APA stylistic guidelines, one does not use the term "poor." The proper term is low-income.

However, low-income is merely a statistical term for a given area. In Rancho Palos Verdes Estates (an affluent community in southern California), low-income means being only able to afford a million-dollar when most homes are two million dollars or more. I will use the word "poor" instead of "low income" because "poor," unlike "low-income," immediately connotes a struggle to meet one's basic needs.

APA guidelines also stress using genderless job titles or job titles that might have negative connotations. For instance, one does not write "garbage men" but instead writes "sanitation workers." However, the term "sanitation workers" is misleading. "Sanitation workers" could refer to workers employed at a water treatment facility. Further, using the genderless term "workers" belies the fact that virtually all "garbage men" are indeed men.

Many occupations, like garbage collector, are lopsided gender-wise. Many more women are employed as nurses than men, and many more men are employed as welders than women. Such gender imbalances are a reality. To ignore such gender imbalances would distort how economic realities affect men and women differently. To recognize gender imbalances, parentheses will be used, e.g., women (and men) will be used when men are in the distinct minority and men (and women) when women are the distinct minority. When the gender balance is very large, such as for parolees or single-parent households, for the sake of simplicity, only one gender is identified. However, nothing in the following chapters is meant to imply a single parent on welfare can't be a man, or a parolee can't be a woman.

Finally, unless stated otherwise, figures cited are for the year 2020.

CHAPTER ONE

A BRIEF HISTORY OF PUBLIC ASSISTANCE AND CAPITALISM

Public support of hospitals predates the Revolutionary War. New York City's Bellevue hospital was founded in 1736. Philadelphia's Pennsylvania Hospital was founded in 1751. New Orleans' charity hospital was founded in 1736 when Louisiana was still part of France. Colonial government accepted there was a moral duty to provide medical care to those who could not afford treatment.

There was also a recognition that government had a moral obligation to care for those unable to care for themselves. Large cities in colonial America had government-funded asylums for the mentally ill. The asylums were more often more like prisons than hospitals, but the poor conditions reflected, in large part, a lack of understanding of mental illness. Even if the custodial care of the mentally ill was often abysmal, at least in theory, government recognized a moral obligation to care for those unable to care for themselves.

Capitalism in colonial America was simple and personal. If a man wanted to borrow money, his personal honor might be his only collateral. An honorable man was expected to pay his debts. If he could not pay his debts, he could be put in a debtors' prison. In a debtors' prison, he would work off his debt. However, prison pay, then, as now, was low. Some languished in debtors' prisons for months, even years, before paying off their debt. Often family or friends had to pay off the debt to liberate their loved ones. George Washington implemented some restrictions on debtors' prisons, and in 1833, Congress completely banned them.

However, workhouses, where a man could find work, have a place to live, pay off debts, and save money, continued. There were also poorhouses that provided shelter for the poor. Poorhouses were privately operated but funded through government contracts. Whatever the owner/operators of government-funded poorhouses did not spend on residents was income/profit. No doubt, many operators were kind and treated residents well while others were more interested in making money. Of course, if a government contract was too stingy, even a well-intentioned owner/operator had to skimp on care. There were also almshouses operated and funded by religious organizations.

In the early 19th century, the Industrial Revolution began, and cities grew rapidly. In 1800, Boston's population was just under 25,000. In 1830, Boston had 61,000 residents. In 1800, the population of New York was about 60,000. In 1830, New York City had over 180,000 inhabitants. In 1830, there were just twenty-three orphanages in the entire United States. By 1850, with the Industrial Revolution in full swing, there were twenty-seven orphanages in New York State alone. Capitalism of the Industrial Revolution brought technological progress, but the price for that progress was more children in orphanages.

From 1861 to 1865, the Civil War raged. During the Civil War, one in thirteen men of military age died, making tens of thousands of women widows and tens of thousands of children fatherless. In 1862, Congress passed legislation that provided a surviving widow of a Union soldier a pension based on her late husband's rank. The moral duty of government to care for the "widow and the orphan" was part of President Lincoln's second inaugural address.

During the Civil War, as medicine was still rather primitive, amputations to prevent gangrene were common. Congress recognized there was a moral duty to assist those who had been maimed while serving the country. A private who lost a limb through amputation received $8 a month (about a third of a month's pay).

The end of the Civil War brought the ratification of the 13th amendment and the abolishment of slavery. The 13th amendment also abolished involuntary servitude, and that meant the end of workhouses. However, poorhouses and almshouses continued.

After the Civil War, the Reconstruction Era began. One particular program of Reconstruction was the Freedman's Bureau. The Freedman's Bureau assisted former slaves to become self-sufficient. The agents of the Freedman Bureau established a variety of programs. They established food programs. They built public schools. They built hospitals. They established Howard, Fisk, and Hampton Universities, the first Black colleges. Black men (and some Black women) could now get a college education, albeit a segregated one.

As America recovered from the Civil War, the number of charities proliferated and grew. The Young Men's Christian Association (YMCA) came from England in 1861 and grew rapidly after the war. Initially, the mission of the YMCA was to bring young men together for bible study. However, the importance of having a healthy body along with a healthy Christian spirit soon became part of the YMCA's culture. YMCAs began having swimming pools and gyms. In particular, the game of basketball was invented at a YMCA to give young men something positive to do during long winters. Nowadays, most YMCAs are simply the "Y" and serve men, women, and families.

Another import from England was the Salvation Army. The Salvation Army came to the United States from England in 1878. The Salvation Army brought the gospel to men who were struggling with alcohol. The Salvation Army still helps those struggling with addiction to alcohol and, now, also helps those addicted to drugs. Today, the Salvation Army is one of the few nonprofit programs that offer residential treatment programs for men as well as women.

Besides the YMCA and the Salvation Army, many other nonprofits were founded in the last half of the 19th century, nonprofits that continue to remain in operation to this day. In 1866, The Society for the Prevention of Cruelty to Animals was established. Eleven years later, the Society for the Prevention of Child Abuse was created. (Yes, animal abuse prevention preceded child abuse prevention). In 1883, Florence Crittenton homes for unwed mothers was founded. Florence

Crittenton closed its last home for unwed mothers in 1981. However, it continues to provide services to teen mothers through community-based programs.

Simultaneous with the increase in the number of charities was a prison reform movement. Many of those advocating for prison reform were acting upon their Christian faith. With the reform movement, prisons became penitentiaries. (The word penitentiary being derived from the Christian concept of penitence). The number of organizations pressing for prison reform and the number of charities was so numerous that in 1872, the first National Conference of Charities and Correction was convened. That same year the Freeman's Bureau was terminated, ending the federal government's involvement in social welfare programs. The needs of former slaves or the needs of the poor of any race were no longer a matter of Federal concern.

Charities, however, could not carry the whole load to care for the poor. States began providing what was referred to as "outdoor relief." In 1899, Massachusetts' outdoor relief program supported around 16,000 individuals at a cost of around $650,000 or a little over forty dollars per person, including administrative expenses. The "indoor relief" of poorhouses continued. However, the number of poor persons living in poorhouses and almshouses was never very large. According to census records, in 1880, there were approximately 66,000 "paupers" living in poorhouses and almshouses. Ten years later, the figure was approximately 73,000.

The late 19th century also marked the beginning of capitalism we know today. In 1870, John D. Rockefeller incorporated Standard Oil (which later became Chevron, Exxon, and Texaco). In 1887, William Randolph Hearst acquired the *San Francisco Examiner*. Hearst went on to acquire or establish newspapers in most major cities. Hearst died in 1951, but the Hearst Corporation still owns several major newspapers, many magazines, and a substantial share of ESPN and A&E networks. In 1892, Andrew Carnegie formed the Carnegie Steel Company, which became United States Steel. United States Steel remains in operation and is the largest steel company in the United States. America used to lead in world steel production. Now, however, United States Steel doesn't even make the top twenty of steel companies worldwide.

Industrial growth of the late 19th and early 20th century was fueled in large part by the sale of stock. In 1882, as a way to report on financial markets, Charles Dow, Edward Jones, and a third man, Charles Bergstresser, established the Dow Jones Industrial Average (DJIA). The three men needed a way to report on the market to meet newspaper deadlines. In an era when mathematical calculations were done by hand, averaging all the stocks everyday would have been very challenging. Thirty stocks were picked to represent the market.

For its first few decades, the DJIA was stable. Then in the 1920s, the DJIA went up and up. It increased by more than twenty-five percent or more in 1924, 1925, and 1927 and increased by nearly fifty percent in 1928. Then the crash of 1929 hit, and the Great Depression began. Millions of men were thrown out of work. (During the Great Depression, the number of women working actually rose from 10.5 to 13 million).

During the Great Depression, to avoid the indignity of begging, some men stood on a corner, holding a sign "apples for sale." The image of a man selling apples on the street corner became one of the iconic images of the Depression Era. In the 21st century, a common sight on freeway off-ramps in southern California is a man, usually Hispanic, selling oranges.

To help put men back to work during the Depression, the Work Progress Administration (WPA) was established. Through the WPA, nearly eight million men (and some women) found jobs. While sometimes ridiculed as "make work" projects, the WPA built many well-known structures, such as the Hoover Dam and Mt. Rushmore. Officially, ninety-six men died in the construction of the Hoover Dam. The actual number is widely believed to be in the hundreds. Several dozen men (the actual number is unknown) who worked on Mt. Rushmore died after they developed silicosis, a lung condition caused by the dust they inhaled dust during construction.

Besides the better-known WPA, a smaller program, the Civilian Conservation Corps (CCC), was developed especially for young men.

Through the CCC, 300,000 men, ages 18-24, were put to work planting trees, building fire breaks, and so on. The young men in the CCA program were required to send two-thirds of their income back home to support their families, whether that family was their parents or the mother of their children.

The Depression also brought the Federal government's involvement in welfare. In 1935, the Aid to Dependent Children (ADC) program was created. ADC replaced the hodgepodge of state welfare programs. Through ADC, the states administered welfare programs, but the Federal government paid a third of the benefits. The Federal government capped its contribution to $18 per month for the first child and $12 for every additional child. A two-child family received a maximum of $90 total or about $550 in 2020 dollars. Under ADC, caseworkers were only authorized to release funds to "suitable families." Given the tenor of the times, it is not surprising that poor, nonwhite families were less likely to be considered "suitable" than poor white families.

In 1934, the Social Security retirement program was established. Prior to Social Security, some elderly quite literally lived out their lives in the poorhouse. In 1939, survivor's benefits for spouses (with the wife almost always being the beneficiary) were added to the Social Security program. So, in practical terms, if a man died, his widow received Social Security, but if a man walked out on his family, his children could get ADC. ADC was much less generous than Social Security. Financially, the widow was much better off than a woman with children.

The Modern Welfare System:

<u>Cash aid:</u>

Over time, ADC morphed into AFDC or Aid to Families with Dependent Children. Under AFDC, the mother, along with her children, was aided as well. So, in government-speak, a two-child family became a family of three. In 1952, the federal government began requiring states to collect child support from the absent parent (almost always from the father). In 1975 states were required to computerize their collection efforts. Today, in most, but not all states, the first fifty dollars collected in child support goes to the mother. In other states, the father's entire child support payment goes to the government.

In the early sixties, the War on Poverty began. In 1962, the federal government paid two-thirds of the AFDC grant, but the states could set the amount of the grant based upon the cost of living in their respective states. Each state paid one-third of the grant and administered the program. In his 1964 state-of-the-union address, speaking of the newly created AFDC program, President Johnson declared, "Our aim is not only to relieve the symptoms of poverty, but to cure it and, above all, to prevent it."

The Federal government set down rules which states had to follow when dispersing AFDC funds. States were required to deny benefits if the recipient refused to accept work except for "good cause." Good cause included having children at home. It was not until 1971 that mothers with children years six or older were required to find work. So, until 1971, on a practical basis, for the mother to get benefits, she just had to prove that she was poor, prove that her children were hers, and prove that her children were US citizens. In 1988, the age level to exclude the mother from having to work was dropped to age three, but there was an "escape clause," the mother and her children could continue to receive assistance if child care to allow the mother to work was not available.

While AFDC mandated work, many saw AFDC as simply a government dole. As long as a woman had at least one child under the age limit, she could stay at home and avoid working for a living. Moreover, while most families on welfare were white, African-Americans and Hispanics were overrepresented on welfare rolls. Further, in many cities, there were large nonwhite neighborhoods where government support easily exceeded income generated by the private sector. There were similar pockets in rural (largely white) America, but being rural, there were not as easily noticed.

Twenty-eight years after President Johnson declared his War on Poverty, in his State of the Union Address, President Clinton proclaimed, "We have to end welfare as a way of life and make it a path to independence and dignity." In the years between Johnson and Clinton, the number of children on welfare rolls rose from 3.2 million to 9.3 million.

Two years after his State of the Union address, President Clinton signed the Personal Responsibility and Work Opportunity Reconciliation Act (PRWORA). With PRWORA, work requirements were tightened. The mother (or single father with children) was expected to work thirty hours a week. If the child or children were fortunate to have both parents in the home, thirty-five hours of work was required. However, the work requirement was waived if the mom or dad was in school or a vocational program. Benefits were also limited to five years. Also, the age limit to be exempted from having to go to work (or attend school) was tightened to six months for a first-time mother and three months for all subsequent children. Also, AFDC was renamed TANF (Temporary Assistance to Needy Families).

Over a period of years, welfare checks went digital. Instead of paper checks, recipients are now given debit cards. At the beginning of the month, the correct amount is electronically loaded onto the recipient's debit card. (Incidentally, paper checks going into unsecured mailboxes at the beginning of each month made for tempting targets for thieves).

With TANF, the federal government recognized that not every adult on welfare could work. With proper documentation, a caseworker could grant an exemption for reasons other than education/vocational training. An exemption could be granted if the recipient had suffered a major illness or was seriously injured in an accident. (It can take months, if not years, for a disability claim to be approved by Social Security). A mother (or father) could also be exempted from having to work if they needed to stay home to care for a severely disabled child. There were also specific regulations for granting an exemption if domestic violence had occurred.

Those granted an education or vocational training exemption usually attend a local community college. Like other colleges, community colleges often require students to successfully complete an introductory course before enrolling in an advanced course. Typically, the introductory course is offered in the fall semester and the advanced course in the spring. For instance, if a welfare recipient is interested in becoming a mechanic, they could enroll in Auto Shop I in the fall and Auto Shop II in the spring. However, the one-year limit assumes the recipient went on welfare right at the beginning of the fall semester. If a recipient went on aid toward the end of the fall semester, it would be several months before Auto Shop I was available. Because the education limit being just one year, the education exemption would be exhausted before the recipient even had an opportunity to complete Auto Shop II.

Within the one-year limitation, a woman on welfare might become a CNA (Certified Nurses' Assistant). (Over ninety percent of CNAs are women). As a CNA working full-time, she will make about $27,000, not a huge sum of money but above the poverty level. The mother has learned a marketable skill, and seemingly "the system" has worked as it should.

However, let's contrast the way the government paid for her to become a CNA with the way the government pays for a new bridge. The government agency responsible for the construction of the bridge announces it is accepting bids, and after the bidding process ends, government officials review the bids. Let's say one company bids ten million dollars to build their bridge and states their bridge will last twenty years. However, another company's bid says they can build the bridge for twenty million dollars, but their bridge will last sixty years.

Contrary to popular belief, government contracts are not necessarily awarded to the lowest bidder. There is usually a clause in the bidding process which allows the appropriate government agency to reject inferior bids. Therefore, a government agency in charge of bridge-building can reject an inferior bid for the cheap bridge and authorize building the longer-lasting twenty-million-dollar bridge, a bridge that will make better use of taxpayers' money.

With how the government accepts and rejects bids for bridge construction, let's relook at the mother, who, as a CNA, is now earning $27,000. She is still living close to the poverty level. She and her children still qualify for food stamps as well as government-funded health care. If she has school-aged children, her children qualify for free school lunch. With her modest income, her family also qualifies for public housing and subsidized child care or daycare. Further, making just $27,000, she pays minimal federal income tax. In cold economic terms, after granting a one-year exemption for the mother on welfare to become a CNA, the government hasn't even built a ten million bridge. It is still paying for ferry service.

However, if the educational exemption allowed her to earn an AA degree and certification as an X-Ray technician (over seventy percent of X-ray technicians are women, and an AA degree is usually required), she would truly be self-supporting. As an X-Ray technician, she could earn $62,000 a year. She would be solidly middle class. Her family would not be on food stamps; her children would not receive free lunch at school. The mother, instead of being dependent on food stamps, etc., would pay her fair share in taxes.

For fathers on welfare, let's take a look at a male-dominated profession, such as welding (over ninety percent of welders are men). An individual can become a certified welder in one year. An experienced welder working in a major company can earn $50,000 or more a year. However, most welders work part-time and earn far less; there is just so much welding a local economy needs.

If the father could earn multiple vocational credentials, not just be certified as a welder, he would be far more employable. If welders aren't being hired, he could do air-conditioning repair; if there is little demand for welders or air-conditioning repair. Having completed Auto Shop I and II he could become a mechanic. A two-year exemption would allow him to obtain multiple vocational certificates. With multiple certificates, instead of a single certificate, the chances of the father finding work and being able to support his children without government assistance are greatly increased.

Food Programs

While food assistance programs existed prior to the War on Poverty, the Food Stamp Act of 1964 solidified the federal government's role in addressing hunger in America. Now, as in 1964, a family's food stamp allocation is based on household size and household income. That is, the allocation for a family of four is the same whether the family is: A mom and three small children, a mom, a dad, and one child, or a mom with three teenage boys. In 2018, the allocation for a family of four was $465. A budget of $465 a month for a family of four can stretch only so far, especially if there are teenage boys in the home. Foodbanks, especially at the end of the month, do brisk business.

Under the food stamp programs, some households are a "household of one," such as a disabled person or a senior citizen living alone. Nine percent of food stamps recipients are over the age of sixty, and most of them live alone. In 1996, when Clinton spoke of "ending welfare as we know it," there were under twenty-seven million Americans receiving food stamps. By September 2018, thirty-four million Americans received food stamps, an increase of 27 percent.

Food stamps, like welfare payments, have gone digital. Now with a debit card, the recipient buys food at the supermarket without the embarrassment of using actual stamps. At the beginning of each month, like with TANF, a debit card is loaded with whatever amount a caseworker has told a state computer should be the correct amount. (If the recipient is also on cash aid, the food stamp allocation is loaded on the same card). Until computers were reprogrammed, many supermarkets reported that on the last day of the month, after eleven p.m., there was a surge of customers. Customers were loading up their shopping carts to be ready to check out right after midnight when funds showed up on their debit card.

Complementing the larger food stamp program is the school lunch program. In 1989, the school lunch program served 9.7 million students. In 2019 it served 20.1 million students -- a more than a hundred percent increase. In addition to the school lunch program, there is also the school breakfast program.

Lesser known than the school lunch and breakfast programs is the WIC (Women, Infant, and Children) program. WIC can provide supplemental nutrition for pregnant women, infants, and children under five. (While the regulations say WIC can serve children up to age five, it has been your author's experience that WIC rarely serves children who are more than a year old). On WIC, a pregnant woman can receive pre-natal vitamins, cheese, and other nutritious food. After she has her child, she can receive a breast pump at no charge. If her child is on formula, she can receive free formula, formula which would otherwise cost a substantial portion of her food stamps allocation. (Formula can be purchased with food stamps). In 1989 there were 4.1 million children on WIC. In 2019, there were also 6.3 million children on WIC, an increase of approximately fifty percent.

Public Housing:

In 1985, as part of the War on Poverty, a cabinet-level agency, housing, and Urban Development (HUD), was created. With money from HUD, many large public housing projects were constructed. The goal of these large public housing projects was to house as many poor people as efficiently as possible. Your author has been in several public housing projects. Many, especially the older ones, look like something out of Stalinist Russia. The walls are painted in drab colors. There is minimal landscaping. Such housing projects look more like institutions than a place to raise a family.

Besides housing projects, the government provides housing for the poor through a voucher program. With a voucher, a sufficiently poor family can – using government money --- rent in the private sector. In

1993, a total of just over 4.06 million Americans were in government-funded housing. In 2016, the total was 4.69 million, or an increase of fifteen percent.

For much of the past two decades, federal regulations have increasingly given priority in housing to the disabled, the elderly, and veterans. From 1993 to 2016 the population of the United States grew by twenty-four percent. With the increase in population and the changes in regulations favoring the disabled, veterans, and seniors, the chances of an income eligible family with children receiving housing assistance is roughly two-thirds of what it was in 1993.

Now, as in 1965, a strong majority of poor families do not live in government-financed housing of any type. Where do they live? They live in apartments where the rent is sixty percent or more of their income. Or they double up with relatives or friends. Or they live in converted garages or other marginal housing. Or they live in homeless shelters or out of their cars. Without a place to call home, such families are deeply entrenched in poverty. For them, the bridge is still out.

Capitalism, social welfare programs, and the need for change

In the latter part of the 20th century, Woolworths and Montgomery Wards, companies that had weathered the Great Depression, went out of business. Other companies founded in the 19th century, like Kodak and Sears, filed for bankruptcy and are shells of their former selves. Both Sears and Kodak were once considered "blue-chip" companies. They were on that very exclusive list of the thirty companies that comprised the Dow Jones Industrial Average (DJIA). Sears was delisted from the DJIA in 1999, and Kodak was delisted in 2004.

In the forty years from March 1939 to March 1979, the membership in the Dow Jones Industrial Average changed only four times. From March 1979 to August 2020, the membership Dow Jones Industrial Average changed seventeen times. Market forces and the fast pace of technological innovation have resulted in modern capitalism being much more dynamic than the capitalism of the past. This dynamic is great for the consumer but not so great for job security.

Technological progress and the global economy are reflected in the number of patents issued and to whom they have been issued. In 1964, when President Johnson's declared War on Poverty, sixty-six thousand patents were granted by the US patent office, and only eighteen percent of those patents went to foreign companies. In 2019, 391,000 patents were granted, and fifty-two percent went to foreign companies.

Similarly, in 1964, several different US companies manufactured television sets in the United States. In 1993, Zenith shuttered the last television factory operating in America. Zenith was later taken over by LG electronics, a Korean company. The demise of the manufacture of television sets in the United States is emblematic of the decline in US manufacturing in general.

Because of technological progress and market forces, both foreign and domestic, compared to past generations, more Americans, through no fault of their own, will, sometime during their working careers, be unemployed. To get by, they will apply for unemployment benefits and other social welfare programs such as food stamps. Providing unemployment benefits and other social welfare benefits to the unemployed, instead of collecting taxes on wages, is a strain on government budgets. Further, the unemployed do not contribute to Social Security, hastening that program's expected financial shortfall.

In 1965, the population of the United States was 194 million, and less than forty-one million were living in poverty. In 2019, the population of the United Sates was 328 million, and forty-seven million Americans lived in poverty. Even with the program of War on Poverty, millions more are living in poverty than in 1985. The "supply" of public assistance programs never catches up with "demand."

Most poor people are not criminals, but poverty and crime are interconnected. If the supply of decent-paying jobs is high, the appeal of "easy money" from criminal behavior is low. However, if there isn't work and one has nothing to lose, looking for "income" through extra-legal means can seem like a rational decision.

Most crime is committed by men, young men, young men who, disproportionately, are nonwhite and poor. Young men without a decent-paying job. Young men who didn't get the education they needed to compete in the 21st-century labor market. Change is needed in the educational system to bring racial and gender equality in high school and college graduation rates.

Good social policy also means providing incentives for greater availability of child care, financial rewards for the poor to obtain preventative medical care, and self-financing retirement plans for modest-wage earners.

Moreover, social policy for the 21st century also needs to encourage a new mindset. A mindset that before starting a family, parents should have the financial stability to support a child without the "child support" of social welfare programs. Also, whether or not they have a decent-paying job, too many men are uninvolved as fathers. Modifications in social policy are needed to encourage men to be better fathers and be more actively involved in their children's upbringing.

Social welfare policy in the 21st century also needs to recognize a simple fact, the physical size of the United States has not changed. Cities and states have not grown in size along with their populations. Schools, buses, subways, roads, city, state, national parks, etc., are more crowded than ever. Rational and effective social policy must recognize that population growth comes much more from the poorest one-fourth of Americans than it does from the richest one-fourth.

Just as modifications are needed in social welfare programs, 21st-century capitalism needs to change with the times. With each passing decade, the rich get richer, and the ability of those with "regular, honest jobs" to have an affordable place to live and otherwise provide for their families becomes harder and harder. So that capitalism serves the greater good various tax incentives and tax disincentives are needed. Healthy capitalism is needed for America to stay competitive in the global economy of the 21st century. However, capitalism that is immoral is not an American value. Everyone, from those living in the most impoverished community to the CEOs of Fortune 500 companies, should have a good moral compass. Sound social policy needs to include promoting ethical behavior.

CHAPTER TWO

WORK ETHIC, MORAL COMPASS, DADS, AND EDUCATION

In the last half of the 19th century, one of the most influential and prolific writers was Horatio Alger. Alger wrote over a hundred novels, and more than twenty million copies of his books were sold. All his novels told the same basic story: An impoverished young man, through hard work, and living in the land of opportunity that was the United States, broke out of poverty and lived a comfortable lifestyle. Living a wholesome lifestyle and "working hard" was the epitome of the Protestant work ethic. (Alger himself was an ordained Presbyterian minister). Even though the young men in Horatio Alger's stories never became wealthy, his books became known as "rags to riches" stories.

Much of the culture of the late 20th Century and early 21st Century is defined by the actions of entrepreneurial young men. Men like Bill Gates, Steve Jobs, Jeff Bezos, and Mark Zuckerberg. However, unlike the "hard-working men" of Horatio Alger's stories, these men were not born into poverty. They grew up in middle-class/upper-middle-class homes. Homes in safe neighborhoods with safe schools. Had they had been born into poverty, it is highly unlikely they would have had the means to create Microsoft, Apple, or Facebook. Also, unlike the young men in a Horatio Alger novel, these young men, like Andrew Carnegie, John Rockefeller, and William Randolph Hearst, before them became enormously wealthy.

Throughout history, individuals born into poverty have rarely catapulted into the wealthiest strata of society. Still, a few beat the odds. One such man is David Steward. David Steward is one of the five

African-American billionaires in the United States. Steward's father worked as a mechanic and took other jobs to support David and the rest of the family. As a child, Steward remembers the fight to have the community pool desegregated.

With his father's encouragement, Steward went to college. After college, Steward landed a steady job – a Horatio Alger-type job – with Federal Express. However, after a few years, Steward left Federal Express to form his own company. With the assistance of the Small Business Administration, Steward won a government contract for his new company. This critical "helping hand" was a significant factor in Steward becoming a billionaire. Besides the critical assistance from the small business administration, Steward credits his success to a supportive father and faith.

A more famous African-American billionaire is Oprah Winfrey. Oprah was born in abject poverty in rural Mississippi. When Oprah was still quite young, her mother left to find work in the North and left Oprah in her grandmother's care. Oprah's grandmother used the Bible to teach Oprah how to read. At age six, Oprah was reunited with her mother. However, by the age of seven, Oprah was back living with her father. She was later returned to her mother's care, where she was sexually abused by a male relative. As a young teenager, Oprah rebelled against her mother and returned to her father's home.

Oprah's father was a steadying influence and pushed her to do well in school. Oprah went to college and began a promising career in local broadcasting, a Horatio Alger job. With faith in herself, Oprah left the "Horatio Alger" job to host a talk show program in Chicago, and the rest, as they say, is history. Like Steward, Oprah credits much of her success to the influence of her father and her faith in God.

Oprah, like David Steward, Bill Gates, Steve Jobs, and Mark Zuckerberg, and the financial titans of prior generations are talented individuals. They didn't "work hard" in the same way as the young men in Horatio Alger's stories, but they put in enormous effort to achieve what they wanted to achieve. However, by definition, most people are of average talent, and while most people take pride in their work, few have the drive of a Bill Gates, a Steve Jobs, or an Oprah Winfrey.

A young man living in poverty, with mediocre natural talent, an average or less than average drive to succeed, no vocational skills, and with just a high school diploma (if that) might be drawn into finding "employment" in illegal activity such as drug dealing. In my experience as a child welfare social worker, if a parent was involved in drug-dealing, it was most often the absent father.

A young woman living in poverty, with mediocre natural talent, an average or less than average drive to succeed, no vocational skills, and just a high school diploma (if that) might find employment in a "Horatio Alger job" such as a health care aide or as a waitress. (Nearly ninety percent of health care aides are women. Seventy percent of all servers are waitresses).

However, if a woman, without any post-secondary education or vocational training, and with little or no desire to work in a legitimate low-wage job, wants to make "real money," she might consider "employment" in some sort of sex-related occupation such as stripper, prostitute, or "webcam girl." Worldwide the adult webcam industry is valued at ten billion dollars. It is estimated that as many as one-third of "cam girls" worldwide are American women. A woman working steadily on an adult webcam or as a stripper can legally and safely earn two to three thousand dollars a month. A man with little education, no vocational skills, etc., earning two to three thousand dollars a month as a drug dealer risks a lengthy prison sentence.

What keeps a poor man or poor young woman with average or less than average talent, average or less than average drive, little education, and no vocational training from seeking employment in illegal activity or a sex-related vocation? They have some sort of moral compass.

How do they require a moral compass? They develop (or fail to develop) a moral compass by how they were raised. In hundreds of ways, large and small, adults in a child's life should impart the importance of being "a good person." The imperative for parents to instill in their child a moral compass is even enshrined in law; the juvenile version of the Miranda rights includes the question "who taught you right from wrong?"

Parents know too well that there are only so many hours in the day. After doing all things (getting the kids ready for school, cooking, laundry, etc.) that *have* to be done, teaching moral behavior is often a rushed job of redirecting unwanted behaviors (e.g., "don't hit your brother" "share your toys," etc.) not installing in their child a clear moral code. If there is just one parent in the home after the "must do" tasks are done, there is even less time to help the child internalize moral behavior.

For the single parent (which almost is the mother) who is poor, it is even more difficult. If she is worried about overdue rent, unsure if the food stamps will last the month, or if there are enough quarters in her purse to do laundry, it is an even greater challenge to instill in her child a virtuous and coherent belief system. Despite these challenges, some in poverty do an excellent job teaching their children right from wrong, and most do at least an adequate job.

Rich or poor, the parents' job of instilling a moral compass in their children is easier if a family is connected to a faith. To use a military term, faith can be seen as a "force multiplier." A "force multiplier" has power in its own right and enhances the effectiveness of something else. A connection to faith – any faith – enhances the ability of moms and dads to develop a moral compass in their children. In my thirty-four career in child welfare, only a very, very small fraction of cases came from families with a long-standing connection to any organized religion.

In past generations, church attendance was a mainstay of the weekly routine. Sunday morning, "almost everyone" went to church. The moralizing influence of faith is, of course, is still present in some communities. Particularly in African-American communities, church is not merely a place to worship; as Oprah Winfrey and David Steward could attest, church is a part of the fabric of life.

However, among all racial groups, church attendance is a fraction of what it was generations ago. Sunday school (and its equivalent in other religions) has seen a dramatically similar decline. A child that does not receive formal moral instruction will, as an adult, likely have fewer qualms about breaking the law or engaging in immoral behavior. (Immoral behavior would include things like raising drug prices to exorbitant levels or paying executives several hundred times more than the average worker). How can children learn the importance of moral behavior while preserving the separation of church and state?

One way is to change how religion is taught in schools. There is an imbalance in how religion is taught. For instance, as part of World History classes, high school students are taught the basic tenets – the moral underpinnings -- of Islam. So, for a quiz on Islam, a teacher might ask what are the seven pillars of Islam or what did Muhammad do? Sensible questions, no different than a quiz on Wilson's fourteen points, or what did Washington do during the Revolutionary War? However, if a teacher were to lecture on the teachings of Jesus, the teacher might be accused of promoting Christianity. This double standard needs to stop. The secular students of today need to learn the basics of Christianity, along with the basics of Islam.

Also, just as schools promote racial tolerance by celebrating Black History Month, Hispanic Heritage Month, and so on, there should be a "Great Religions of the week." A "Great Religions of the World Week" could include clergy as guest speakers from differing faiths. For many students, this would be the first time they would hear from the clergy of any faith.

Of course, morality and religion are not synonymous. Ethics can be taught without direct reference to religion. The Center for Philosophy of Children (CPC) at the University of Washington promotes such a program. It has a program that teaches, in a non-religious manner, ethics at the senior and junior high school levels. CPC also organizes an annual High School "ethics bowl" competition. A student who earns a trophy in ethics will likely lead an ethical life as an adult.

Of course, many adults with no connection to an organized religion lead ethical and moral lives, and some supposedly devout, including clergy, have engaged in immoral behavior. However, it is fair to say that if you randomly selected ten thousand people who attend worship regularly and randomly selected ten thousand that never attend worship services, the crime rate in the latter group will be higher.

Houses of Worship help build what urban planners call "social cohesion." Neighborhoods with high "social cohesion" have a lower crime rate, while bars and liquor stores do not add to social cohesion and attract crime. In part, because they provide social cohesion, Houses of Worship are exempt from paying property taxes, while zoning laws can limit the number of bars and liquor stores.

Most of the larger religious denominations have substantial charity programs. For instance, there is a Catholic Charities program in most major cities. The Catholic Charities of Galveston-Houston alone has a budget of forty million dollars! Forty million dollars that are *independent* of the local diocese's budget for church-related expenses. There is also Lutheran Services, Jewish Family Services, and similar organizations that do "God's work" for those in need. Contrary to common perception, as verified by independent organizations, the vast majority of faith-based (as well as secular) charities are very responsible and efficient with their money.

Community programs, whether organized by a nonprofit or operated by local government, can change lives. One mother on my caseload had a particularly long history of drug use. She had many failed attempts at rehabilitation. She began turning her life around when a friend asked her to join a church softball team. Similarly, a father in my caseload credited his participation in a city-sponsored baseball program for helping him remain "clean and sober" and reassume custody of his children.

One community program that has received national attention is the Dance Theater of Harlem. The Dance Theater of Harlem opened in 1969 and has helped thousands of girls (and some boys) learn to dance, particularly ballet. Some of their students, as adults, have found professional careers in dance. However, the real story is teaching the value of a work ethic and a belief in oneself. A work ethic and a belief in oneself do not guarantee upward mobility from "rags to riches," but without a work ethic and a sense of purpose, upward mobility is highly unlikely.

How then to build social cohesion, ethical behavior, and a work ethic? Like with many things, money helps. Specifically, money that would otherwise go to the expensive bureaucracy of government could be more efficiently used by charities. Tax policy, therefore, should incentivize contributions to local nonprofits. For a taxpayer in the twenty-five percent tax bracket that itemizes, a three hundred dollar donation to a charity costs only $225. However, until recently, for the ordinary taxpayer who didn't itemize, a three hundred dollar donation cost $300. There was no tax break for the not-so-affluent to be charitable.

Things got a little bit better in 2020. Now, an ordinary taxpayer in the fifteen percent tax bracket can deduct the first $300 given to charity. So, a three-hundred dollar costs $255. However, if the same taxpayer is particularly generous and makes a thousand-dollar contribution to charity, the cost for the deduction is $955. However, for the affluent taxpayer in the twenty-five percent tax bracket, a one thousand dollar donation costs only $750. Much social cohesion could be accomplished if ordinary taxpayers could deduct donations to nonprofits in their county of residence.

Such a deduction could pump billions into community programs. Yes, there would be some loss in revenue, but the government already *loses* significant revenue by giving corporations tax breaks for doing business in "empowerment" or "enterprise" zones (empowerment zones and enterprise zones being government-speak for impoverished neighborhoods). Giving tax breaks to corporations to do business in impoverished communities is a "top/down" mindset of "help the corporation to help the needy." When it works, that's great. However, when it doesn't work, it is a waste of taxpayer dollars.

An additional way to help impoverished communities would be to allow contributions made to nonprofits operating in empowerment or enterprise zone to be considered tax *credits,* not just deductions. Allowing such credits would encourage the affluent to funnel money where it is needed most. Further, for the not-so-wealthy living in empowerment zones, getting a tax credit for even a modest donation to a local nonprofit would help residents invest in bettering their communities and build social cohesion.

To help build better communities, the federal government does have student loan forgiveness programs to encourage teachers and health professionals to work in impoverished (aka underserved) communities. Typically, for each year the professional (doctor, nurse, teacher, etc.) works in an impoverished community, a certain percentage of their student loan is forgiven. However, doctors, nurses, and teachers do not create wealth. Capitalism creates wealth. *All* college graduates working in an impoverished community, whether they work for a nonprofit, a small business, or a corporation, should have a percentage of their student debt forgiven each year. Such a student loan forgiveness program would encourage those with business or technical skills to bring their skills (and work ethic) where they are needed.

The Importance of Dads:

Hundreds of academic studies corroborate what Oprah Winfrey and David Steward said about their fathers, fathers are important. Unless the father is abusive or has an active substance abuse problem, when the father is in the home with the mother, children are more likely to graduate high school. They are more likely to pursue education/training after high school. If the father is in the home, teenagers are less likely to become delinquents or, as adults, become criminals. Further, a girl who has a healthy, loving relationship with her father is less likely to become pregnant as a teenager, and a boy who grows up with "a good father" is less likely to get a girlfriend pregnant. Finally, boys and girls who grow up with two loving parents are more likely, as adults, to be part of a two-parent family. Like with faith, having a dad in the home is a "force multiplier."

There are also "economies of scale" when mom and dad live together versus the father being out of the home. Say a family of four's combined household income is a modest thirty thousand dollars, an amount just slightly above the poverty level. Also, let's say this thirty-thousand-a-year family is lucky and pays only forty percent of their income in rent (many poor families pay a much greater percentage). After rent, our two-parent, two-child family has $18,000 a year for non-rent-related expenses. If the father is not living in the home, there are two rents to pay, two sets of utility bills, and so on. If the father's rent is forty percent and the mother's rent is also forty percent, now, instead of a family of four trying to live on $18,000 (after rent), two households try to live on $6,000.

In California and other states, high school students are required to pass a semester of economics. Along with teaching traditional economic principles, high school economics classes need to teach the economic benefits of a two-parent household. To some, that would be preaching morality. However, ignoring the economic benefits of a two-parent would be denying a mathematical truth.

State laws vary considerably regarding how much the absent parent (aka the father) must pay in child support. However, generally, child support hinges on the amount of custody time, the number of children, and the relative earnings of each parent. In years past, until some child support caseworker calculated the amount, neither the father nor the mother knew how much child support the father would pay and how the mother would receive. Now, some states have websites with a child support "calculator." A couple contemplating a separation can now consider the financial ramifications first.

As any parent knows, children want their own space. They want a place to put their stuff, play video games, watch Netflix, or just hang out with friends. Ideally, each parent should have about the size of the household. If the mother has a two-bedroom apartment, then the father needs to have a two-bedroom apartment. However, if the father can only afford a studio apartment, his children naturally will be less inclined to visit. If the father has less custody time, his child support order can increase. Even if the father has liberal visitation, a child support order of thirty-five percent of his income is not unusual. If the father pays forty percent of his income in rent and thirty-five percent in child support, seventy percent of his income is gone before he pays for food and other necessities.

What might he do to get by? He may take an under-the-table cash job. Working a cash job, he pays no taxes, and no child support is garnished from his wages. By working a cash job, he effectively gives himself a healthy promotion. However, employers who pay cash want to be invisible. They don't provide verification of employment to landlords, credit card companies, or legitimate employers. Moreover, employers who pay employees in cash don't contribute to Social Security. The failure of the cash-basis employee and the cash-basis employer to pay taxes on earnings adds to the federal deficit and Social Security's projected shortfall.

Many of the fathers in my caseload worked at under-the-table cash jobs. Or, more commonly, they cycled between cash jobs, legitimate odd jobs, and being unemployed. Some of these men were on relatively good terms with the mother of their children. If she found herself low on diapers, low on groceries, or needed a small appliance, he helped her out. Of course, not every absent father provided in-kind support. However, when fathers provided such "in-kind" support, their children saw them in a more positive light. Their children were emotionally healthier. Emotionally healthier children are more likely to become emotionally healthy, economically self-sufficient adults.

Early in my career, several fathers who had been out of work for months reported that when they landed a legitimate job, their *entire* first paycheck was garnished. A few fathers reported that after deductions for health insurance, they even had negative paychecks! Now, at least in California, the garnishment of wages for child support collection is capped at 65%.

In one of my first child welfare cases, I was assigned to investigate a report of a dirty home. The mother, we'll call her Tricia, lived in a one-bedroom apartment with her ten-year-old son, Cameron. While many parents are hostile when a cps social worker knocks on their door, many, like Tricia, are actually quite cooperative. Tricia recognized that her apartment needed serious vacuuming. She explained that several weeks before, her vacuum cleaner broke, but she couldn't afford a new one as she was already behind in rent. (It hadn't occurred to her to repair the vacuum cleaner herself, as, in her words, "that was a man's job.")

However, being without a vacuum cleaner for weeks was not the real issue. The real issue was her ten-year-old's behavior. Because of Tricia's work schedule, Cameron had a couple of hours alone to himself each day. During these times, Cameron often got into trouble with the neighbors or skipped school, and even when his mother was home, he resisted doing chores, taking a shower, brushing his teeth, and so on. Tricia felt, and I agreed, Cameron needed a father figure. However, her son hadn't seen his father in years. As far as Tricia could tell, Cameron's father quit working as soon as child support collection caught up with him. Presumably, with his paycheck being completely garnished, there was no reason for Cameron's father to work at a legitimate job.

In most states, for "cooperating" with child support collection, a mother on welfare receives the first fifty dollars of the father's child support. Any additional child support collected from the absent parent (aka the father) goes to the government. In other states, *all* the child support collected from the father goes to the government.

Even in states where the welfare mother receives fifty dollars from the father, the mother might not realize the father is paying child support. Just so many dollars are loaded up on her welfare debit card each month. From her financial perspective, the man she once loved is quite literally "good for nothing." She may openly express her resentment of her "good for nothing" ex-husband or ex-boyfriend, or, for the benefit of her children, she may try to stifle her resentment. However, even if she has the best intentions to do otherwise, some resentment will likely seep through. This makes the father's job to be an involved father that much harder.

In a "generous" state like California, a woman on welfare with two children receives a little over $800 a month-- an amount way, way below the poverty level. One simple way to alleviate poverty would be to treat children on welfare like other children and have child support go directly to the mother – not the government. If a woman on welfare receives child support, she will be more inclined to have a civil relationship with the father, and the children will see their father in a more positive light. Further, it would encourage fathers to seek legitimate, honest employment because they are assured the garnishment of their wages is going for *their children* and not government coffers.

Wouldn't government coffers feel the "pinch" of this lost revenue? Not really. Child support collected to offset the cost of welfare is a revenue stream so small, so obscure, it is virtually undetectable in government budgets. It is money that could be missed. But for a mother on welfare, trying to make do on $800 a month, a few extra hundred dollars a month in child support makes a huge difference. She can buy clothes for her children at Kohl's or Old Navy instead of at a thrift store. If her child is sick and needs to go to the doctor, instead of taking the bus, she can give gas money to a friend who has a car. If her vacuum cleaner breaks, she can afford to buy a new one.

Whether he lives in the home or not, a man who is a good father will carry some of the joy of being a father into his workplace. A good father is more likely to be a good employee. Conversely, the inept father or hot-tempered father is likely to be a less desirable employee. Without the government trampling on individual rights, how can the government help the absent father be a better father and, by extension, a better employee?

When the police issue a traffic ticket, in most states, there is a financial incentive for the ticketed driver to complete a state-approved driving school program. Of course, completing a safe driving course is no guarantee a driver will become a safe driver, but averaged over tens of thousands of drivers, the frequency of unsafe driving is reduced. Similarly, not *every* parent who completes a government-approved parenting course will become a better parent, but the chances are better if they do.

Of course, many will say, "the government isn't going to tell me how to raise my child." As a child welfare social worker, I heard the objection, "no one will tell me how to raise my child," many, many times. Yet, nearly every parent in my caseload who completed a required parenting course as part of their treatment plan told me they learned something of value. Also, already in California, in family (divorce) court, when a couple separates, there are strong incentives for the mother and father to (separately) complete an approved co-parenting program. However, this program focuses on avoiding the ill-will that often accompanies a divorce (or unmarried separation) and not the struggles of day-to-day parenting.

What can the government do to encourage the absent parent (aka the absent father) to complete a parenting program? A program that the father will likely be resistant to attend but ultimately would find beneficial. Just like with driver's education classes for traffic violations, a financial incentive is needed. The absent parent could be given a five percent discount on child support if he (or she) completes an approved parenting program. Does this rob the mother of money to which she would otherwise be entitled? Yes, but she gains for more than she loses. For the vast majority of women, a five percent reduction would be worth every penny if, in return, she got a more capable co-parent. If she can count on the father to do his share in raising the children, her stress is reduced. She is happier and is more likely to be a more productive employee herself.

Of course, for fathers and mothers to adequately provide for their children, they need good jobs. Good jobs require getting a good education. For a child that lives in a poor family, getting a good education is a challenge. In the nation's two largest school districts (New York City Public Schools and the Los Angeles Unified School District), eighty percent of the students come from poor families, and the dropout rate is nearly twenty-five percent!

Nationally, boys are *fifty percent* more likely to drop out of school than girls. The gender discrepancy is even greater for children of minorities. In 2016, 95.5 percent of African-American girls graduated high school, but only 88.7 percent of boys. For Hispanics, the gender imbalance was slightly better (91.3 v. 88.6).

Educators can do little about the social ills, poverty, crime, substance abuse, absent parents, etc., that affect school performance and attendance, but they can choose how to teach. In most school districts, three or four years of English are required for graduation. However, high school English is most often taught as literature. Historically, that has been the literature of dead white men: Shakespeare, Steinbeck, F. Scott Fitzgerald, Hemingway, and so on.

The authors of books assigned in English classes are now more racially diverse than in the past. However, English classes still focus on *fictional* literature. Adult women count for nearly *eighty percent* of all novels sold, so presumably, high school girls, much more than high school boys, enjoy their fiction-heavy English classes than do boys. Moreover, one of the very few nonfiction books commonly assigned in English classes is a diary written by a girl. Her name was Anne Frank. Of course, Anne Frank's story is important for both boys and girls to know, but girls naturally will relate to her much more than boys.

When teaching literature, high school English teachers will often ask questions like: What did the author mean? How did the author employ foreshadowing? How did such and such character change over the course of the novel? And so on. Learning about character development and such are excellent skills for future screenwriters and playwrights (and future English teachers) but little else. Only a minuscule number of high school students will go onto careers where an understanding of *fiction-writing* is required.

High schools need to place a greater emphasis on teaching students how to write nonfiction -- *the type of writing that is needed in the business world*. To learn how to write good nonfiction means reading good nonfiction. Boys (and many girls) will find Robert Donovan's story of Kennedy and PT-109 or Trevor Noah's *Born a Crime* far more interesting and readable than Steinbeck or Shakespeare. Of the four years of English typically required of high school students, at least one year should be devoted to nonfiction.

Also, a semester of (non-religious) ethics should be required. An ethics class like those offered by the University of Washington. Imagine what a better society we would have if students spent a semester learning ethics instead of studying poetry, character development, or plotlines.

Fictional literature, even that of "dead white men," of course, still has a place in English classes. However, it needs to be taught in a manner that boys (and girls) find socially acceptable. Social standing is critical for high school students. It is something they will protect at almost any cost. For students, the socially safe thing is to show contempt for anything that isn't considered "cool." Shakespeare and Steinbeck are generally not considered "cool." If a boy shows interest in something that isn't cool, he risks being mocked by his friends. However, if he clowns around and the teacher sends him to the office, he has maintained his social standing.

Many schools now routinely track students sent to the office for disciplinary reasons. Using such records, your author would like an APA (American Psychological Association) style study to see how frequently boys misbehave in "feminine, fiction-heavy," English classes compared to other subjects.

How can the classics of English literature be taught in a way that students, particularly African-American boys, find socially acceptable? It shouldn't be too hard to get male celebrities, such as Shaquille O'Neal, or Samuel Jackson, to do YouTube videos featuring recitations of Shakespeare and other classics. An English teacher could show such videos either in class or require viewing as part of a homework assignment. If Nick Fury (Samuel Jackson) recites Shakespeare, then Shakespeare is cool.

Changes are also needed outside the classroom. Almost all school districts now have websites. Typically, these websites, among other things, post demographic information about the school district, the total number of students enrolled, the number of ESL (English as a second language) students, graduation rate etc. However, if a school district posts its graduation rate, it is rarely broken down by gender, but as noted, boys are much more likely to drop out of high school than girls. Federal regulations (commonly referred to as Title IX provisions) require schools to ensure gender equality in educational opportunities. Title IX needs to be invoked to require every school district to post on graduation rates, by gender, on their websites.

CHAPTER THREE

FOOD PROGRAMS AND HOMELAND SECURITY

Government food programs for the poor are not new. In ancient Rome, bread was given away as part of holiday festivals or as a way for the emperor to demonstrate his benevolence. Other times food was distributed to keep the peace, emperors being quite aware that a hungry mob can become an angry mob.

Throughout much of history, food has been used as an instrument of war. Invading armies would lay siege to a city to starve the inhabitants into surrender. The modern world has tried to be more civilized. The Geneva Convention specifically states that prisoners of war must be provided with sufficient nutrition and that failing to provide food to a prisoner is considered a war crime.

However, there is one demographic group in the United States, a group that is over ninety percent male and disproportionately nonwhite, that is not accorded the same decency as a prisoner of war. In many states, a man (or woman) on parole, no matter how poor, is ineligible to receive food stamps. In some states, even after a parolee has demonstrated a law-abiding lifestyle and is discharged off parole, the food stamps ban continues. Three states (South Carolina, Mississippi, and West Virginia) even have a lifetime ban! If denying an enemy prisoner food is a war crime, how can America morally justify denying a parolee who is otherwise eligible from receiving food stamps? Moreover, studies have shown that denying food stamps increasing the chance of a parolee reoffending and returning to prison, which in the long costs the state even more money.

As indicated in chapter one, food stamps have gone digital. A mom on welfare checking out at the supermarket no longer has to pull out a booklet of stamps with a line of customers looking on and judging. Food stamps, however, didn't go digital out of concern for the recipient's possible embarrassment. They went because digital stamps are cheaper and easier to process than actual stamps. Debit cards instead of paper stamps have dramatically cut down on fraud. Paper food stamps that could be sold for cash. Cash that could be used to purchase alcohol or illegal drugs or cash for necessities like diapers, toothpaste, laundry soap, or non-prescription medication.

Neither food stamps nor Medicaid pays for non-prescription medication. If food stamps haven't lasted a month out, a food bank might help out. However, if you are poor and you or your child has a headache, an upset stomach, or a sore muscle and there is no money to replenish the medicine cabinet, it means just having to tough it out.

One nine-year on my caseload, we'll call him Johnny, lived with his mother, whom we will call Mary. Johnny started having serious stomach pains, so Mary made an appointment with a pediatrician, the same pediatrician Johnny had when he had been in foster care. However, Mary didn't have a car. Getting to the appointment by bus would require a transfer and take ninety minutes, a trip that, by car, would take less than thirty minutes. Further, the bus stop was a couple of hundred yards from the doctor's office. Johnny wasn't well enough for such a long walk. Mary asked me to take her and her son to the appointment, and I did so.

After the physical exam, the doctor spoke with Mary and me. The doctor provided his diagnosis and advised a combination of over-the-counter medications. Mary, however, asked for a prescription instead. The doctor assured Mary that any over-the-counter medications would be just as effective as any prescription. Still, Mary looked bewildered. The doctor gave me a quizzical "what is going on?" look. I asked Mary if she had enough money for the medication. She did not. I believed her. Still, Mary still felt it necessary to open her purse to show the doctor and me that she had a single dollar bill and a lit bit of change to last the three days until the end of the month. I agreed to buy the medication for Johnny. (Only very reluctantly did the county provide reimbursement).

With Johnny and Mary in mind, one wonders how many mothers on Medicaid, like Mary, have asked a doctor to write a prescription when an over-the-counter medication would do. Or, when food stamps were actual stamps, how many were "fraudulently" sold for cash for medication for a sick child, diapers, or other legitimate need.

The dollar value of food stamps a recipient receives is based on family size and income -- the same way it has always been calculated. There is no adjustment for the ages of the children or gender. A teenager needs more calories than a toddler. A teenage boy needs more calories than a teenage girl. A physically inactive teen boy needs about 2,000 calories a day, but if he is active in sports, he may need 3,200 calories (a girl active in sports needs about 2,700).

Boys and girls who participate in sports are much more likely to graduate from high school. Moreover, by playing sports, boys and girls develop a sense of teamwork and responsibility, virtues valued in the modern workplace. Further, a well-fed child is more apt to be a better-behaved student. Surely, in the 21St century, it shouldn't be too difficult to reprogram government computers, so a family's food stamp allocation is adjusted to ensure teenagers, particularly boys, have sufficient calorie intake.

Some have argued that food stamps should be contingent upon recipients finding employment. Such pleas show ignorance of the food stamp program. Of the thirty-eight million Americans on food stamps, forty-four percent are children. Twenty-one million more are the parents of those children and are already subject to TANF's work requirement rules. Another thirty-three percent are the disabled or elderly. That leaves a paltry two percent.

Of course, some part of that two percent includes bums on the street, panhandling for booze. However, even the alcoholic needs to eat. The morally right thing to do, despite the bum's alcoholism, is to feed him. (Food stamps cannot be used to purchase alcohol). Without food stamps, the bum will have inadequate nutrition. Coupled with his abuse of alcohol, the bum will likely develop serious health problems. He will need medical care, possibly very expensive medical care, medical care paid for by taxpayers. Simply put, the bum that receives food stamps is a healthier and cheaper bum. From both a moral viewpoint and an economic viewpoint, no one in America, not even the bum or the parolee, and certainly not the teenage boy, should go hungry.

School lunch program

The national school lunch program reimburses local school districts to provide free or reduced-fee school lunches. Free meals are provided to students whose families earn less than 130 percent of the poverty level. Reduced fee meals are offered to students whose household incomes are between 130 and 185 percent of the poverty level.

The ratio of students receiving free meals to reduced meals is roughly eight to one, suggesting that the reduced fee program is greatly underutilized. Using census data, it shouldn't be too hard to estimate the number of moderately poor (130 to 185 percent of the poverty level) students that live in a given school district. To increase the number of students utilizing the reduced-fee lunch program, school districts could be given a modest financial incentive. A few million dollars to encourage good nutrition is a small price to pay for having better-fed and better-behaved students. The 2019 budget for the school lunch program was just under twelve billion dollars.

Like food stamps, school lunches have gone digital. The days of a lunch lady consulting a list of names on a clipboard regarding who does or does not qualify for a free lunch are gone. Whether on the free lunch program or paying for lunch, after getting their meal, the student enters a code at the "cashier." If the student does not qualify for free lunch, the appropriate amount is deducted from the student's account. Of course, not all parents remember to keep money on their child's account. Negative balances accrue, perhaps simply because the parents forgot to pay. Of course, other times, because they have been laid off, had unexpected medical bills, or some other financial hardship, parents didn't pay because they didn't have the money.

School districts, of course, have to pay the vendors that supply food to schools. With budgets tight, some school districts have engaged in "food shaming." Food shaming is when a child with an unpaid balance is given a meager lunch (or no lunch at all) while other students get the regular lunch. California and other states, however, have banned the practice. Food shaming should be banned nationwide.

Similar to free lunch is the free/reduced fee breakfast program. Many school districts do not offer free breakfast because it means staff has to come in early for "yard duty" in the cafeteria. Depending on the size of the school and the children's habits, there could also be the additional cost of providing custodial staff to clean up after breakfast. Further, the free breakfast program is underutilized because of the realities of bus schedules. Just over half of all students take a bus to school. School districts can't provide two bus services, one for children who eat breakfast and another for those who don't.

To encourage school districts to offer school free breakfast, school districts should be given a modest (e.g., twenty-five cents per breakfast) financial incentive to cover the additional costs of "yard duty" and custodial staff. For a million children, such a program would cost about forty-four million dollars or about half the cost of a single F-22 fighter jet. The 2019 budget for the breakfast program was nearly four and a half-billion dollars. A few extra million to incentivize school districts to use the school breakfast program would be money well spent.

Just like their more affluent counterparts, teenagers from poor families are apt to sleep in and skip breakfast. Of course, the earlier in the day the school day starts, the more likely students are to skip breakfast. A strong body of research shows that starting the school day later helps students do better both academically and behaviorally. Based on this academic research, effective in 2022, in California, middle schools can start no earlier than 8:00 a.m. and high school no earlier than 8:30 a.m. This change alone will help graduation rates and help decrease poverty in future generations.

Lunchtime, especially in high school, is a social time for students. In many schools, but particularly at affluent high schools, most students do not eat in the cafeteria. They either bring their lunch or are free to leave campus to get lunch at a nearby fast-food restaurant or convenience store. The poor student who qualifies for free lunch may choose to socialize with more affluent classmates than eat in the cafeteria. The pain of feeling left out can be greater than the pain of hunger.

As most people know, school lunches and school breakfasts have to meet nutritional standards set by the Federal government. Obviously though, a nutritious meal that is unappetizing goes uneaten. To get students, rich or poor, to eat a nutritious meal school districts should seek student input into cafeteria menu selection. This could be particularly effective in poorer school districts. Junior and senior high school students could vote on their favorite meals, getting one vote for each meal. Each vote would be a chance to win a monthly prize of, say, fifty dollars. For a poor student, a chance to win fifty dollars is substantial motivation. For the meager sum of fifty dollars a month, a school could see a meaningful increase in poor students eating lunch.

WIC (Women, Infant, Children)

Brain development begins before birth and continues at a fast pace in the first few years of life. (Brain development, at a much slower pace, continues into early adulthood). An infant or toddler that does not receive good nutrition can suffer permanent brain damage. Similarly, a pregnant woman who is undernourished will likely have a baby with sub-optimum brain development.

Recognizing the importance of good nutrition for pregnant women and young children, the federal government created the WIC (Women, Infants, and Children) program. Through WIC, a sufficiently poor woman, if pregnant, can receive free prenatal vitamins and vouchers for healthy food. A mother with a young child, through can receive vouchers for food, vouchers for formula, and a breast pump free of charge.

To receive the benefits of WIC, the mother has to prove to a government official that she is sufficiently poor. (Age-eligible foster children qualify regardless of the foster parents' income). The budget for the WIC program is 5.3 billion dollars. Given that good nutrition is critical for prenatal and postnatal brain development, funding WIC is certainly a worthy use of taxpayer dollars.

While morally justified and economically prudent, the WIC program reveals a sad fact. *Sixty percent* of all infants in the United States are income-eligible for WIC, meaning *nearly two-thirds* of the children in America are born in poverty or near-poverty. America cannot prosper if two-thirds of its children are born in poverty or near poverty. How to discourage poor families from having a child they cannot afford to raise is addressed in chapter seven.

WIC is often administered by the county health department. As a social worker, I've found the staff at health departments exceptionally well-dedicated, but the waiting areas for public health offices, like government offices almost everywhere, are exceptionally utilitarian. The chance that a woman too affluent for WIC would visit an institutional-looking public health clinic to get vouchers for baby formula or a free breast pump is nil.

Far, far more likely, is that, for whatever reason, a poor mother is unable to prove she is sufficiently poor, and she and her young child are unable to receive good nutrition through the WIC program. As the chance of WIC fraud is extremely low, but the benefits of serving *every* needy woman and infant critical, income verification for WIC should not be required. The savings from not having to pay the expenses of caseworkers to document poverty would easily outweigh the infinitesimally small number of affluent women who would go out of their way to receive a modest government benefit.

United State Department of Agriculture (USDA)

To consumers and farmers alike, the mission of the USDA concerns food production, food safety, and animal husbandry. Yet, the food stamp program is the largest line item in USDA's budget, and the school lunch program is the second-largest. However, of the men (and one woman) who have been cabinet-level secretaries of the Department of Agriculture, only one, Alfonso Epsy, had any particular experience in anti-poverty or hunger prevention programs. The rest had ties to farming or ranching, were previous members of Congress, or had other political connections. Expertise in crop yields and animal husbandry (to say nothing of political connections) does not translate into expertise in assuring the poor have enough to eat.

The Department of Health and Human Services (HHS), which administers TANF (aka AFDC) and most other anti-poverty programs, is the logical government agency to administer food programs. Having welfare programs under one roof will result will, over time, result in considerable cost savings. Application forms can be consolidated, duplication in computer systems avoided, and so on.

Homeland Security, immigration, and food production

In most countries, a child's citizenship is based upon the child's parents' nationality, not where the child happens to be born. However, in the United States, a child born in the United States automatically becomes United States citizen. US citizenship is highly prized. The value of US Citizenship is such that even some affluent pregnant women have engaged in "birth tourism." Birth tourism is when, on a tourist visa, a pregnant woman lawfully enters the United States to give birth. Her child automatically becomes a citizen of the United States. The child's American citizenship being a hedge against possible political upheaval in the mother's home country.

However, most attention has been on poor women coming to the United States to give birth. Some refer to the children of such women as "anchor babies." Meaning, in part, the child serves as an anchor for the rest of the family to stay in or come to the United States. However, very few pregnant women make the arduous trek across the border.

Sixty percent of those apprehended by Southwest Border Patrol are single adults, the vast majority of which are men. Most of the other forty percent apprehended by the Border Patrol are intact families. A tiny number are unaccompanied minors, usually teenage boys. According to the World Bank, twenty-nine billion dollars is "remitted" to Mexico every year. Presumably, much of that twenty-nine billion dollars remitted to Mexico comes from who entered the United States without the necessary documentation.

If a woman is pregnant when she crosses the border or if she becomes pregnant after she crosses the border, as noted, when her child is born, her child becomes a US citizen. The mother can apply for public assistance programs for her newborn. The mother will not receive any benefits herself but can, on the child's behalf, receive food stamps, cash aid, and her child will have taxpayer-financed medical care. Because of privacy laws, when she applies for benefits, the caseworker will not report her to immigration. Once the paperwork is in order, the caseworker enters the data into a state computer, and the aid is dispensed accordingly to the non-citizen mother on behalf of her citizen-child.

During my tenure as a social worker, I had several cases where the older children in the family were Mexican nationals while the youngest children were born in the United States and were US citizens. The younger children qualified for assistance programs, but the older children who were Mexican nationals did not. (Incidentally, if a child is removed from the home due to maltreatment, child protective services is required to contact the appropriate consulate, but other than this provision, the child's nationality is generally irrelevant).

While caseworkers are assuring that assistance is properly dispensed to the citizen-child through the non-citizen mother, officials at the Department of Homeland Security (DHS) are tasked with deporting those who illegally entered the country. Seemingly, the left and the right hands of government are working at cross-purposes. Yet, if Homeland Security deported the mother, the father, and older siblings for lack of US citizenship, that would mean breaking up the family. Breaking up a family merely because of citizenship seems unconscionable.

Still, it seems ludicrous that tax money (in the form of cash aid, food stamps, and medical benefits) is provided to someone who entered the United States unlawfully, even if such assistance is for the benefit of a citizen-child. Further, without proper documentation, the non-citizen parent, unless using false documentation, pays no income tax on earnings — taxes which could offset the government assistance their child was provided. Is there no middle ground between breaking up families and have non-citizens act as conduits for government benefits?

There is. Welfare regulations could be written so that effective on such and such date, noncitizen applicants would need to designate a US citizen as the conduit of benefits. The US citizen could be a trusted friend or relative. The trusted friend or relative would be expected to disburse the assistance to the mother (or father) to support the citizen-child. Adding the trusted person requirement would discourage many from entering the United States illegally. To discourage fraud, the trusted friend or relative would be subject to criminal prosecution if funds were not properly disbursed. Further, if the supposedly trusted person proved unworthy, the non-citizens in the household would be protected from deportation.

The responsibility to enforce immigration law relies primarily with the Department of Homeland Security (DHS) and its subsidiary agencies, the Department of Border Patrol (DBP) and Immigration and Customs Enforcement (ICE). ICE is feared by many US Citizens of Hispanic heritage. They fear that in an ICE raid, they will not be able to prove their United States citizenship and be deported by mistake -- an ordinary state driver's license not being proof of citizenship. However, a driver's license that meets DHS standards ("a Real ID") that allows an individual to board a plane can be sufficient to prove citizenship. One wonders how many US citizens of Hispanic descent but don't plan to fly have obtained a Real ID.

Many of the men and women who enter the United States without proper documentation find work in agriculture. Working in agriculture is physically demanding. Typically, farm laborers are not paid by the hour but by piece rate; so many pounds of produce equals so many dollars. Of course, as the years go by, advancing age affects the farmworker's ability to earn a living, and fewer pounds of produce harvested means less income. Eventually, the body can take no more, and the farmworker, who entered the United States illegally, possibly decades ago, retires and becomes dependent on family. As this nonworking, non-citizen gets older, their need for medical care, often expensive medical care, increases -- medical care that greatly exceeds their ability to pay.

As indicated in chapter one, in the 18th and 19th centuries, local tax money was used to keep a city's hospital financially solvent when patients were unable to pay. Hospitals in the 21st Century are not so lucky. If a poor, non-citizen needs medical treatment, there is usually no government program to pay for the patient's care. In 2017, twenty-seven hospital *chains* declared bankruptcy. In 2018, it was ten hospital chains; in 2019, it was twenty-two hospital chains. Of course, medical care for indigent non-citizens is not the only cause for a hospital chain to go bankrupt, but surely, especially in the Border States, it is a contributing cause.

In 2009, the Department of Homeland Security formed the Food Protection and Defense Institute (FPDI). The FPDI is concerned with protecting the food chain from the effects of epidemics, natural disasters, terrorist attacks, and similar calamities. The FPDI is not the least bit concerned about farm labor immigration (legal and illegal) on food production. Yet, as the pandemic showed, maintaining a reliable food chain is a matter of national security.

Even before the pandemic, the American Farm Bureau (AFB) reported that the current work permit program (the H-2A program) was inadequate in supplying enough farm workers. Food went to waste, and farmers lost income. How then to assure there are enough farmworkers to bring in America's harvest?

The answer lies in history. During WWII, there was a shortage of farm labor. Because of this shortage, Mexico and the United States signed an agreement that seemed, at least on paper, to be fair. Under the agreement, a Bracero (Spanish for farmworker) was guaranteed pay for each day worked, a daily stipend for when he did not work, as well as free health care and free housing. Upon his return to Mexico, the Bracero received a very substantial "end of contract" bonus. Sadly, when many Braceros returned to Mexico, no "end of contract" bonus was provided as promised.

Despite the need for farm labor, during the war, only several thousand Mexicans participated in the program. The Bracero program, however, continued. In 1956, there were 445,197 Braceros working on US farms. The Bracero program ended in 1964.

Today with modern banking, money can be sent internationally, cheaply and instantaneously. With modern media, news crews could quickly report if farmworkers were not being paid as they should. With proper oversight, Bracero version 2.0 could be a win-win situation. A win for the farmer needing labor, a win for the American taxpayer, and the Bracero, working legally in the US, would not fear deportation, and upon returning to Mexico be reunited with his (or her) family in Mexico, and receive the end-of-contract bonus.

CHAPTER FOUR

PUBLIC HOUSING, CRIME, AND HOMEOWNERSHIP

The first public housing project was Techwood, a WPA project. Techwood opened in Atlanta, Georgia, in 1936. While not opulent, Techwood had what was then considered "modern conveniences" such as gas and electricity. Also, unlike so many public housing projects of the future, Techwood had parks and other spaces, as well as a recreational area and a health clinic. Techwood provided homes to 604 families at the cost of 2.7 million dollars (or $49 million in today's dollars). After decades of crime, especially drug trafficking, Techwood was razed to provide housing for athletes for the 1996 Olympic Games.

Techwood was not the only public housing complex to be torn down because of crime. One of the largest public housing projects was Pruitt-Igoe in St. Louis, Missouri. Completed in 1956, Pruitt-Igoe was a massive complex of thirty-three eleven-story buildings. Pruitt-Igoe cost $33 million to build ($306 million in 2019 dollars). In part, because the elevators did not stop at every floor, there were frequent robberies and assaults in its hallways. Pruitt-Igoe was dynamited into oblivion in 1976.

Other housing projects shared a similar fate; in Chicago, a complex of public housing units called Cabrini-Green, at its peak, housed 15,000 individuals. Because of criminal activity Cabrini-Green became known as "little hell." Most of the Cabrini-Green complex was torn down in 2011. Another ill-fated housing development was The Magnolia Projects in New Orleans. Magnolia Projects had 1400 units and had one of the city's highest murder rates, a city with an already high murder rate. The Magnolia Projects met its demise from Hurricane Katrina and was not rebuilt.

It wasn't until 1996 the federal government acted on the connection between high-density public housing projects and crime. In 1996, convicted sex offenders were banned from public housing, as were those convicted of selling methamphetamine. A conviction for any serious crime, including being under the influence of an illicit substance such as methamphetamine could also mean a denial of public housing. However, if an applicant had completed a drug rehabilitation program or needed housing to allow for family reunification in a child welfare case, the applicant could request an administrative review to plead her case. On behalf of several mothers (it was never a father or a couple), your author has participated in such administrative reviews.

In 2005, interim regulations were enacted to protect domestic violence victims from discrimination. However, as an example of the government's slow pace, the final regulations regarding domestic violence and public housing were not adopted until eleven years later.

As noted in chapter one, instead of building large public housing projects, federal policy has increasingly relied upon vouchers for the poor to obtain housing in the private sector. Because of how the Federal government codifies its rules, such subsidized housing is often referred to as "Section 8."

Like those in public housing complexes, under Section 8, recipients pay one-third of their household income in rent and a local housing authority, with federal money, pays the rest. As with public housing complexes, applicants are screened for criminal records. Slowly, because of regulations regarding criminal record checks, public-supported housing became safer or, more accurately, less dangerous.

There is an inverse correlation between the cost of housing and crime. In more affluent areas, there is less crime, particularly less violent crime. There is also a statistical correlation between race and crime. Cities with larger nonwhite populations have a higher crime rate than cities with smaller nonwhite populations. For example, in Detroit, the median cost for a home is a very modest $53,000, and in 2019 its murder rate was 40 per 100,000 residents. In 2019, in Baltimore, the median home price was $152,000. Its murder rate was 55 per 100,000 residents. Nearly two-thirds of the resident of Baltimore and over three-quarters of residents of Detroit are African-American.

Contrast Detroit and Baltimore with Irvine, California, and Scottsdale, Arizona. The median cost for a home in Irvine is $753,000, and the median cost for a home in Scottsdale is $433,000. Irvine's murder rate is less than one per 100,000 residents; for Scottsdale, it is less than two per 100,000. Irvine and Scottsdale have a minimal number of African-American residents.

However, individuals with college degrees rarely commit violent crime, and violent crime by doctors, lawyers, and similar professionals is close to nil. In Detroit, only fifteen percent of residents over twenty-five have a college degree, and close to twenty percent did not graduate high school. In Baltimore, it is slightly better, with thirty-two percent having a college degree and "only" fifteen percent without a high school diploma. In Irvine, *two-thirds* of the residents over the age of twenty-five have a college degree, and the high school dropout is close to zero. For Scottsdale, a little over *sixty percen*t of adults over twenty-five years old have a college degree, and the high school dropout rate is very low.

Historically, African-Americans have been underrepresented in college. Now African-American women attend college at about the same rate as their percentage of the overall population but only about a third of African-Americans in college are men. The gender divide for African-Americans continues in most professional schools; fewer African-American men entered medical school in 2014 than in 1978. For law schools, the gender disparity in favor of African-American women to African-American men is similarly unbalanced. Other professions are even more unbalanced; for every male African-American man that is a psychologist, there are nearly six African-American women. If more men, particularly African-American men, were able to become college graduates, as well as doctors, lawyers, psychologists, and other professionals, America's cities would be safer.

As African-American men, as boys, are less likely to graduate high school, it is not surprising that African-Americans are over-represented in prison populations. (Education is, of course, not the only cause for this disparity. Numerous studies show that, even for the same offense, African-Americans are more likely to receive a more severe sentence). Roughly one-third of the Federal prison population is African-American or approximately three times their percentage in the overall population. The racial disparity is even sharper in state prisons. In some states, African-Americans are the majority of the prison population. In South Carolina, the ratio of African-American inmates to white inmates is roughly four to one. In Mississippi, it is three to one, and in West Virginia, three and a half to one. In states with relatively few African-Americans, the disparity is even greater. In Maine, it is six to one. In Vermont, ten to one.

A 2003 Department of Justice found that only 11 percent of inmates in state prisons and 24 percent of inmates in federal prison had any post-high school education. A 2017 report from the National Center of Education Statistics showed that nearly a third (29%) of inmates scored level 1 or 2 on math or literacy (Level 3 is considered a basic level of competency. Level 4 is considered proficient).

Incarceration is expensive. At the federal level, the cost to operate Federal prisons is just over seven billion dollars. The Federal prison serves slightly more than 150,000 inmates or a cost of about $47,000 per inmate. Incarceration at the state level is, on average, only slightly less expensive than federal prison. Money spent by states for prison means money not spent for state universities and state colleges. Less state money means higher tuition and more student debt for the lawful, pursuing a college degree.

Of course, the cost of violent crime is much more than the cost of incarceration. There is the cost to pay prosecutors, bailiffs, and other court personnel. There is the cost to provide legal counsel to the guilty and innocent alike. There is the expense of medical care for victims. Victims of violent crime, especially those living in poor areas, rarely have private insurance. It is tax dollars that pay for their medical care.

Just one victim of a gunshot or other life-threatening injury can cost the taxpayer hundreds of thousands of dollars for hospital care. Besides hospital care, treating victims of violence can mean paying physical therapists, mental health therapists, and other professionals. Further, the patient/victim might be permanently disabled. If permanently disabled, the victim is entitled to life-long government benefits.

Besides having a sufficiently clean criminal record, applicants for public housing or a section 8 voucher must demonstrate income in the desired range. Too little income and the applicant cannot afford even a one-third share of market rent. With too much income, the applicant isn't considered poor enough to qualify. In both programs, veterans and the disabled have priority, with a disabled veteran having the highest priority. Applicants must be US citizens or legal residents.

Typically, once a Section 8 voucher is issued, the applicant must find housing within ninety days, or the voucher becomes void. (For housing projects, applicants are placed on a waiting list. In high-rent San Luis Obispo County, the waiting list was closed more often than it was open). Even paying one-third of the market rate, finding housing can be difficult. If the recipient has been unable to find a place but has made a good faith effort to find subsidized housing, the local housing authority can grant a sixty-day extension. In San Luis Obispo County, even with the sixty-day extension, and needing to pay only one-third market rent, some parents in child welfare cases were still unable to find affordable housing.

Once the applicant finds a rental unit, a contract is signed. With federal money, the local housing agency guarantees the landlord full market rent. If the full market rent is $1,200 a month, the tenant pays $400. So the government's share for a year's rent is $9,600 or more than the *entire* federal individual income tax of an average tax return. So, in other words, it takes more than one family's taxes to pay for another family's housing. Put another way, the incarceration of one individual in federal prison equals the subsidized rent for four families.

The Section 8 program and a myriad of smaller programs are funded by the federal department of Housing and Urban

Development (HUD). The term *urban development* indicative of the federal government's historical involvement in large-scale housing projects in urban areas. A name change is overdue. Renaming HUD to Housing and Environmental Development (HED) would work. The name would reflect that affordable housing is needed everywhere and that government-funded projects should be built or offered in an environmentally friendly manner.

Those receiving subsidized housing stay in subsidized housing an average of six years (longer in high rent cities like San Francisco or New York, or San Luis Obispo). Of course, many people, particularly the disabled or the elderly, remain in subsidized housing permanently. Only the most diehard libertarian would have qualms about helping the disabled, those too old to compete in the open labor market, or disabled veterans receiving subsidized housing for as long as they need. But what about the "ordinary poor?" Shouldn't there, like with welfare, be time limits for a family to receive subsidized housing? The answer is mostly no.

Ending a rental subsidy after a prescribed period, or more humanely, gradually decreasing the subsidy over years for the "ordinary poor" would *seem* like a reasonable incentive to wean a family off the government dime. After all, if a family had to vacate a rent-subsidized apartment after a specified period, that would free up a unit for another eligible family. However, reality is more complicated.

Cutting off the rent subsidy and forcing financial independence for non-disabled/non-elderly/non-veteran households assumes two things: 1) the adults in the household have the job skills where they can find and maintain employment in a vocation where financial independence is possible, and 2) such jobs are available. With the one-year limit on the education exemption for welfare-to-work, the chances of a welfare recipient acquiring vocational skills to find a "good-paying" job to afford full market rent are slim. Further, as discussed in detail in chapter eight, with technological advances and market forces, there are just fewer good-paying jobs.

Of course, some families do get off public housing. This can happen in many ways. The children grow older and can attend an after-school child care program. With the children in after-school care, the mother (or parents) can work more hours and afford to pay market rent. Other times the mother can work more hours as the abusive father has permanently left the home. Or the mother has a new boyfriend or husband, and with the man's income, the combined household income exceeds government standards for assistance. Acquiring vocational skills that lead to obtaining a good-paying job is another reason, but certainly not the most common.

Let's say that the household income of a family who has "graduated" from public housing is fifty-thousand dollars. In high rent cities, like New York and San Francisco, fifty thousand dollars is well under income limits for housing assistance, but in most of the country, fifty-thousand dollars a year is enough to get by. However, let's say the economy falters, and the parents are laid off. Mom and dad look for work, but the only jobs available are at minimum wage, not nearly enough to pay the rent. On behalf of the entire family, the mom applies for food stamps. With food stamps, the family can eat, but food stamps won't put gas in the tank. Mom and dad apply for unemployment benefits.

Living on unemployment the family quickly falls behind in rent, utilities, car payments, etc. The parents apply for housing assistance, but like before, they will wait *years* before a voucher or a unit in public housing becomes available. Through no fault of their own, they are back in poverty again. Government programs are needed to help needy families *permanently* out of poverty.

Though generally not thought of as such, the housing assistance offered as part of the GI benefits has helped create *permanent* wealth and prevent poverty. The first GI assistance bill was signed into law in 1944. Then, as now, the GI Bill provides two major benefits: Tuition assistance and loan assistance for veterans to buy a home. With tuition assistance, by 1956, 7.8 million veterans of WWII, the vast majority who were men, attended college or received vocational training. With college degrees or vocational skills, these men were able to find good jobs. They were able to provide for their families without further assistance from the government.

The GI bill also helped nearly 2.4 million veterans of WWII obtain housing. Again, the vast majority of recipients were men. Entire communities, like the original Levittown, were established and financed through GI benefits. In 1949, a home in Levittown cost just under $8,000. Today the median cost of a home in Levittown is $400,000. The increase in home value being approximately five times the overall rate of inflation.

Most of the veterans of WWII have died. With their deaths, the equity they established in their GI-bill acquired home passed on to their children. Their adult children reaped the benefits of their father's service. Now veterans of the Korean War, the peace years between wars, and even the Vietnam War are beginning to die off in large numbers. Their children, *through no effort of their own*, inherited equity because of their fathers' service.

With equity in a home, when hard times hit, a family has a financial cushion. If a homeowner falls behind in mortgage payments, they will get demand letters from the bank, but no landlord or property manager will come knocking on the door. Moreover, when a borrower is delinquent, to avoid having to write off a bad loan and to avoid the expenses of foreclosure proceedings, banks will often agree to a repayment plan for past due amounts. However, for legal reasons, many property management companies and owners of apartment buildings will not accept partial payment on past due rent. Simply put, a job loss or other financial hardship is much harder on the tenant than the homeowner.

Recognizing the benefits of homeownership, the Federal government has the FHA program. Typically, an FHA buyer pays five percent as a down payment, so for a two hundred thousand dollar "starter home," including closing costs and other expenses, a buyer needs at least fifteen thousand dollars. For the family earning fifty thousand a year, trying to save fifteen thousand dollars for a down payment is just a pipe dream. They permanently rent. When they die, their heirs have no home to inherit.

For those with better-paying jobs, jobs that require a college degree, saving for a starter home is still hard. The average college graduate has slightly over $25,000 in debt to repay. Saving $15,000 for a down payment is, to say the least, quite challenging when already owing $25,000.

When new homes are built, the builder is assessed various fees by the local government. Traditionally, such fees were meant to cover the expense for a city inspector to verify that a newly constructed home was fit for habitation and other government expenses directly related to the home's construction. Now fees are often added to fund the construction of a new school or other infrastructure needed because of the influx of new residents. In many cities in California, as in cities in other states, building fees also include a surcharge to create a pool of money for the construction of affordable housing. In the City of Fresno, the building fee to fund affordable housing is a whopping $45,000!

How then to encourage a profit-seeking developer to build an apartment complex (with a dedicated park for children) or build detached homes (with a park nearby) for those of modest means? Instead of penalizing developers with fees, reward developers with tax breaks. If the tax codes were amended to allow the developer to earn tax-free profits, a builder would have a significant incentive to build affordable housing earmarked for those a local housing authority deems eligible. To avoid building another Techwood, Cabrini-Green, or Magnolia, the number of affordable units could be capped at, say, twenty percent of any project. So, for a hundred-unit apartment building or a hundred home project, the developer would earn tax-free profits on twenty percent of the units. Using financial incentives ("carrots") is usually more effective than financial penalties ("sticks").

Another way to encourage the construction of affordable housing would be to provide generous tax breaks to major companies that construct affordable housing for their employees. While executives, lawyers, accountants, software engineers, and others with in-demand technical skills can make six-figure salaries at major companies and (presumably) can afford homes, major companies still need secretaries, security guards, custodians, and other lower-paid employees. Providing "carrots" to encourage large companies to build affordable company housing for their employees to buy (not rent) would certainly bring more affordable housing to those who might not otherwise own a home. Imposing "sticks" (aka tax penalties) for large companies that *did not* provide employees an opportunity to purchase owner-occupied housing would also work. A combination of "carrots" and "sticks" would work even better.

Non-profits provide some modest help for housing the poor. One well-known non-profit that helps those of modest means own their own home is Habitat For Humanity. Habit for Humanity helps low-income families all over the world obtain permanent housing (and, by extension, the homeowner's heirs). With Habitat for Humanity, the future homeowner contributes "sweat equity" by helping in the construction of their new home. Through a combination of the eventual homeowner's sweat equity, volunteers, and a paid crew, a new home is built.

In 2018, Habitat For Humanity helped just over 18,000 individuals in North America obtain new or refurbished housing. However, eighteen thousand is a tiny, tiny fraction of the housing needed. One reason so few homes were built is that building homes with inexperienced labor is inherently inefficient. Homeowners and volunteers have to be trained. There is also inefficiency as applicants have to screen, and many, many more apply than are chosen. Time and money are spent on those "not chosen" is time and money wasted.

Further, Habitat for Humanity usually only builds just a few homes at a time. A private developer building a hundred homes can achieve economies of scale that are not possible building a few homes at a time. Further, an experienced work crew working that works steadily is more efficient than an ad hoc crew that has to start anew with each new house. Also, construction workers employed on a large project have a steady source of income for a sustained period. Construction workers working on a series of small projects don't have a consistent income stream. Without a consistent income stream, it is harder to save. Some, especially the younger members of a work crew, likely need homes of their own.

How could a government agency "scale up" Habitat For Humanity to provide consistent jobs for construction workers but avoid the pitfalls of the past with public housing? A local housing authority (with federal dollars) would provide the money, and recipients, like in the Habitat for Humanity program, would contribute "sweat equity" by volunteering in local community programs. However, the actual construction, though, would be left to skilled tradespeople.

Once the eventual homeowner worked the requisite number of hours, the local housing authority would be authorized to release money for a down payment on a home, whether that home is an owner-occupied apartment, a mobile home, a townhouse, or a traditional single-family detached home. Some might say this would create some huge bureaucracy of civil servants tracking down and verifying that volunteer hours were actually worked. However, with little paperwork, many public high schools track students' participation in volunteer work, and once the requisite number of hours has been earned, the students receive special recognition. A huge bureaucracy to track "sweat equity" in community programs isn't needed.

Under a "sweat equity" program, just as the federal government guarantees FHA loans, the local housing agency would guarantee mortgage payments to a lender. There would also be common-sense restrictions on the property. The family would have to live in the unit for so many years before selling to anyone other than another eligible family. Also, just like banks require conventional borrowers, the home would need to be kept in good condition.

Under a government sweat-equity program, if the new homeowner could afford only to make payments on a $100,000 loan, but the home costs $200,000, the new homeowner could be sold a fifty percent share. Years, later when the property is sold, say for $300,000, the owner would get half of the profit or fifty-thousand dollars, and the government would get its money back, plus fifty-thousand dollars. If the owner(s) remained in until their death(s), the heirs would be entitled to a corresponding share of the property. Many heirs would undoubtedly use this money to buy their first home. The cycle of homeownership would continue. Poverty would be averted. The bridge does not have to be built again.

However, while a sweat equity program and changes in the tax code would create more owner-occupied housing, as well as, create social cohesion, reduce crime, and provide for inherited wealth, such changes, alone, would be insufficient to meet demand. Even if a sweat equity program and tax codes changes created ten times the housing built by Habit for Humanity, there still would not be enough to meet current demand, to say nothing of future demand. The supply of affordable housing certainly needs to be increased, but demand also needs to be reduced.

Demand could be reduced if more Americans had decent-paying jobs. However, as discussed in chapter eight, good-paying jobs, especially good-paying jobs which do not require a college education, are harder and harder to find. With fewer good-paying jobs available, the spread between the demand for government-supported housing and the supply of such housing will only grow larger and larger. Those, who in previous generations would have been homeowners, now rent. As they die, there is no equity for their children to inherit. Without action, the divide between the haves and the have nots will only deepen.

CHAPTER FIVE

POVERTY, CHILD NEGLECT, AND CHILD CARE

A sufficiently poor family can receive cash aid, food stamps, and free health care. With food stamps, they are not hungry, with cash aid, they can pay utility bills, and with Medicaid, they can see a doctor without charge. If they are fortunate and have subsidized housing, they can afford to pay rent. Assured of these basics, both the children and the parents in the household are emotionally healthier. Without the constant fear of paying rent, putting food on the table, and keeping the power on, the mom or dad or both are better able to hold down a job or benefit from vocational training that will lead to a better job. Moreover, without having to stress about basic necessities, they will be better parents. Both from being better parents and their children's own increased sense of security, the children will do better in school. As they are no longer living in functional poverty, the *possibility* for upward mobility is significantly increased.

Poverty, it should be mentioned, is sometimes "romanced." Phrases like "we didn't have much, but we had each other" or "money doesn't buy happiness" try to put a positive spin on poverty. However, leave a twenty dollar out where a poor person might find it, and you will see joy come to that person's face. Further, many adults, who grew up poor, can vividly remember the thrill they had the first time they got their own set of clothes and not hand-me-downs.

As a child welfare social worker, I saw first-hand how economic poverty impacted the lives of families. Children who came into juvenile court as victims of neglect, abuse, or domestic violence almost always came from poor families. It is safe to say that four-fifths of children that enter foster care come from the poorest one-fifth of society.

Neglect/child endangerment due to a parent's substance abuse program is the most common reason for a child to be removed from the home. Of course, affluent people abuse drugs and alcohol, but after a night of heavy drinking or drug use, they are still affluent in the morning. There is food in the refrigerator and gas in the car.

In California and some other states, parents in abuse/neglect court cases who can't afford an attorney are represented by a court-appointed attorney. However, in many states, in child welfare cases, poor parents have to represent themselves. This creates a legal absurdity. A poor parent arrested for being under the influence of an illicit substance, facing possible jail time, gets an attorney, but that same parent, who might permanently lose custody of their child, is not appointed counsel. While losing one's freedom is bad, losing custody of one's child is even worse. It just seems morally wrong to consider jail time more worthy of appointed counsel than a parent's custody.

Moreover, from personal experience, I can say that parents in child welfare cases often do not listen to their social worker's advice. However, if they have an attorney and their attorney tells them to seek treatment as recommended by the social worker, the chances they will seek treatment increase dramatically. If they get treatment, such parents are more likely to rejoin mainstream society as taxpayers, saving the government tens of thousands of dollars. Morally and economically, parents in child welfare proceedings should be appointed counsel.

On those rare occasions when a parent was too affluent to be provided a court-appointed attorney, it was almost always was a non-offending, steadily employed father. Typically such a father had not lived with the mother for years. These steadily employed, non-offending fathers usually were granted custody fairly quickly.

Whether the child was released to the father, placed with a relative, or placed in foster care, if the mother was on welfare, her aid stopped. She suddenly went from being poor to being very poor. She likely had no job skills. If she was lucky, she could enter a residential treatment program and, within a month or two, have her child returned to her custody in the residential treatment program. (In my entire career in child welfare, *I have never even heard of* a residential treatment program where children could be placed with their fathers).

Once the mother and child are in a treatment program together, the mother can receive cash aid, though, typically, the treatment program, takes a portion of welfare grant as rent. (While in a residential treatment program, the mother is exempt from welfare-to-work rules). If she doesn't get into a residential treatment program, she risks losing her housing as she no longer has any income. To pay for housing, instead of being a mere drug user, she might look to extra-legal means to support herself or, more commonly, "couch surf," staying with one friend or relative after another. With such unstable housing, her chances of successfully completing treatment are greatly reduced.

In my thirty-fours in child welfare, many parents completed required treatment programs, had their cases closed, and had their parental rights fully restored. When their cases were closed, the majority of these parents were still poor or nearly so. If their child had remained in placement and been adopted by foster parents or relatives, the child, at least economically, would have been better off. Adoptive parents lead law-abiding lifestyles and typically have steady, stable jobs.

However, if the child is not returned to the mother's care, she loses motivation to establish a substance abuse-free lifestyle. She is less likely to obtain regular employment and is more likely to enter or re-enter a criminal lifestyle; in short, she remains an economic drag on government budgets. Further, if her child remains in foster care or the care of a relative (a relative usually on the maternal side), taxpayers wind-up paying foster care/adoption assistance for years.

For the father whose child remains in foster care or the home of a maternal relative, his opportunities to remain a part of his child's life are usually minimal. Even more than the mother, he has less motivation to seek a law-abiding, substance-abuse-free lifestyle and become part of mainstream society.

So from the taxpayer's point of view, it makes sense to offer parents who had the children taken from them a second chance. There is also a moral argument. Allowing for redemption is a basic principle of our nation's Judaic-Christian heritage. (Of course, Muslims and those of other faiths also believe in giving second chances, but the theological basis for doing so is somewhat different).

Like most parents, parents in child welfare cases need affordable child care. I had one case where the mother, we'll call her Anne, lived with her two young children in a two-bedroom apartment. Anne had a history of substance abuse but had been drug-free for some time and was nearly at the end of her formal treatment. Her children were in her care, but with on-going court supervision. Anne and her young children slept in one bedroom of a two-bedroom apartment. A roommate slept in the other bedroom. Anne's only "income" was cash aid (aka welfare) and food stamps. Anne and her roommate were civil to each other, but it was a roommate arrangement born out of mutual financial necessity, not close friendship. Anne and her children desperately needed housing of their own. However, the vacancy lists for public housing and Section 8 vouchers had been closed for years. There were no vacancies in publically-funded housing of any type for Anne, or anyone else, anywhere in the county.

For reasons beyond Anne's or the roommate's control, they had to vacate their apartment. Anne and the roommate parted ways. With money from a relative, Anne bought a small, well-used trailer. Anne parked the trailer in a trailer park. Some trailer parks are quite nice, with a clubhouse, swimming pool, and a park for children to enjoy. The trailer park Anne and her children lived in was not one of those. Her trailer park was just a parking lot with hookups for electricity and water. Yet, the *space* rent for the little slab of concrete her trailer park sat upon was ninety percent of her welfare grant. So, after rent, Anne had less than twenty dollars to pay for diapers, toothpaste, toilet paper, and other necessities. Still, she was better off than the father of the children. For weeks at a time, he lived out of his car. Other times, especially if the weather was bad, a relative took him in, even though it violated the terms of the relative's lease.

Anne wanted to work; however, she had no vocational skills. Any (legitimate) job she found would be at minimum wage. If she found a job, she needed government-funded child care. I completed the appropriate paperwork for her to get free child care, but it was months before such care became available. Once she had daycare, Anne found a job. However, it was too little too late. In the months waiting for daycare to come through, Anne started using drugs again and made other misjudgments. When the depth of her problems became clear, her children were returned to foster care and were subsequently adopted.

Another mom on my caseload, we will call her Tanya, had some job skills. Tanya had a job that paid about four dollars above minimum wage. Tanya and her three-year-old daughter lived in a two-bedroom apartment. With a (relatively speaking) decent-paying job, Tanya could just afford rent. (The father of her child had no job skills, was on probation, and "couch-surfed"). Tanya was fortunate; government-funded child care came through for her just as her child was returned to her care. Still, Tanya had to drive two hundred miles a week to take her child to/from daycare, as there were no other child care openings, with or without government funding available.

Like Anne and Tanya, millions of poor single mothers, a much smaller number of poor couples, and a very small handful of poor fathers rely on government-funded family child care. For those working at the minimum wage, the cost of child care can equal or even exceed their entire income. It would be cheaper for the government to increase the welfare grant by fifty or sixty percent than pay the expense of full-time child care for a young child. But the government doesn't do this. The thinking is that by having the mother join or remain in the workforce, she will become self-sufficient or at least less dependent on government aid. Also, having a job will give the mother purpose beyond her parental duties. She will have greater self-esteem. With purpose, she is less likely to drown her sorrows in alcohol or illicit substances. Also, if she has a job, it is more likely any new boyfriend (and potential stepfather) will also have a job. In short, while government-funded child care is expensive on the front end, it makes for better families and is less expensive in the long-term.

In California, the budget year runs from July 1 to June 30. In San Luis Obispo County, with state and federal money, a local nonprofit administered child programs. Many years, around April, social workers and welfare staff would get an email from the nonprofit agency saying that they weren't accepting any new applications; there were no more state or federal dollars left in that year's budget to pay for child care for any more children. So, a mother (or father) who needed subsidized child care in April, May, or June was out of luck until the new fiscal year on July 1. Something is morally wrong when government benefits are dependent on when, in a calendar year, an applicant seeks assistance.

One well know government program, Head Start, provides child care for preschool-aged children. Head Start was established in 1965 as part of the War on Poverty. The effectiveness of Head Start has been extensively studied by academics. Whatever the academics have to say about Head Start's effectiveness, poor parents of preschool-age children overwhelming desire it for their children. Head Start programs usually operate near full capacity. Parents often have to wait for months for a much-coveted vacancy. Without child care, a parent with a small child cannot find work. A minimum wage job is better than no job at all.

Head Start serves a little over a million children. Its budget is slightly over ten billion dollars. That breaks down to a cost of ten thousand dollars per child or more than tuition at a state college! However, this cost is comparable to child care rates in the private sector. Even in the private sector a year's worth of child care for a preschool aged child can equal (or even exceed) a year's tuition at a state college.

Parents that pay for child care out of their pockets get a tax *credit*. They get a maximum credit of $1,050 for one child and $2,100 for two or more children. In many parts of the country, child care expenses, especially for toddlers and infants, can run $800 or more a month. At eight hundred dollars a month, the annual cost, even with the tax credit, of having two children in child care is a whopping $17,100 a year. On a personal note, when my wife and I had two children in childcare, one evening while watching television an ad came touting the "low cost" to lease a Mercedes-Benz. I remarked to my wife, "Honey, for the cost of child care we could each lease a Mercedes-Benz and still have money left over."

According to Health and Human Services, there are just over 233,000 child care providers in the United States (and as more women have careers, that number has been steadily dropping). More self-pay, and government-funded, child care providers are needed. If the first ten thousand dollars of a child care provider's income were tax-free, that would encourage many stay-at-home moms to earn extra income caring for one (or two children) while caring for their own children. This would increase the overall number of daycare "slots." To increase the number of day care providers receiving government funding, in addition to tax-free earning, providers could receive a tax *credit*, of say, one thousand dollars.

With more child care "slots," child care is closer to home and work. Parents, rich and poor, would have a shorter commute. With a shorter commute, employees will be more likely to get to work on time, and that helps their employer's bottom line. Shorter commutes would be better for the environment too.

The revenue loss from not taxing the first ten thousand income in child care earnings would not be that great. At a fifteen percent tax rate, 300,000 child care providers not being taxed on the first ten thousand dollars of earnings translates to a revenue loss of a paltry 450 million. However, the actual revenue loss would be even lower as with child care, more women (and some men) would be employed, and the government would tax earnings from those jobs.

Whether it is in the form of tax breaks and credits for child care providers or direct government funding payment, parents who pay for child care are understandably envious of their tax money going for child care expenses for someone else's child. Further, if those tax dollars support a child whose parents merely had a "casual arrangement," that envy can become moral indignation. Families struggling to pay their own daycare bills, to pay rent or mortgage, or save for their children's college want their tax dollars go towards things, like road, bridges, or medical research that could be of benefit of everyone. There are over 46,000 structurally deficient bridges in the United States. So many bridges equals so many children in Head Start.

CHAPTER SIX

THE APEX AND BASE OF THE PYRAMID

In 1965, the ratio of CEO's salary in top companies to that of the average worker was twenty to one. In 1989, the ratio of CEO salary to the average worker was fifty-eight to one. In 2018, it was a whopping two hundred and seventy-eight to one. Similarly, in 1995 the wealthiest one percent owned less than twenty-five percent of all wealth. In 2016 the top one percent owned over a third of the wealth. The apex of the pyramid is getter richer, much richer.

Income taxes are supposed to be progressive. Those at the top of the apex not only pay more but proportionally more. The tax rate tables reflect. According to 2019 tax tables, for married couples, the first $19,750 they earn is taxed at ten percent; anything they earn over 622,000 is tax at 37%. Before President Trump's tax rate reform, the top tax rate was 39.6 percent.

The affluent itemize their taxes and benefit from a variety of deductions not available to the less affluent. Itemizing their deductions, the affluent can deduct large charitable contributions and deduct mortgage interest. The affluent also benefit from depreciation schedules, the oil depletion allowance, and a host of other tax-reducing rules. In practice, the rich often do not pay a fair share. As billionaire Warren Buffet has repeatedly stated, he pays, on a percentage basis, less tax than his secretary.

Rich people, like Buffet, invest in stock. There is no sales tax on the sale of stock. We have federal excise taxes (excise tax just being a fancy name for sales tax) on the things ordinary people buy, like gasoline, alcohol, and cigarettes. Why not tax something the rich buy? If a couple "invests" in their child's physical and emotional health by buying a two-hundred-dollar bicycle for their child, they pay sales tax. But if William Buffet buys two million dollars' worth of stock, he pays no tax. Moreover, if an affluent person sells stock at a loss, the loss can be used as a deduction. However, if, at a garage sale, the parents sell that $200 bicycle their child has outgrown for twenty-five dollars, there is no deduction for the loss in value of the bicycle.

In the United Kingdom, the sales tax on stocks is one-half of one percent. A tax of one-half of a percent sales on shares sold on NYSE and NASDAQ would generate about thirty-eight billion dollars. A half of one percent tax on the sale of stocks would encourage true investing versus pure profit-taking. Most trades on stock exchanges are computer-generated, so a tiny change in a stock's price can trigger an automated buy or sell order. With a tax on the sale of shares, a stock would have to have a meaningful gain before it would make sense to sell. This would encourage genuine investment over a pure profit motive. A financial market with a mindset of long-term investment, instead of a mindset of pure profit-making, helps companies retain employees and prevents poverty.

When a stock is sold at a profit, there is a capital gains tax. From 1954 to 1967, the maximum capital tax rate was a steady twenty-five percent. Since 1967 the rate has gone up and down dramatically. In 1972, it was 35 percent. In 2003 it was just fifteen percent, with several different amounts in between. In 2020, the rate was twenty percent for a married couple earning more than $488,000. A return to the historical rate of twenty-five percent is overdue. Taxing the affluent selling stock at twenty-five percent, a higher rate than an ordinary taxpayer pays on wages, is fair because if the stock is sold at a loss, the affluent person can deduct the loss. Granting a tax deduction for selling stock at a loss is, in essence, a government subsidy for a poor business decision.

Imposing a luxury tax on those who buy yachts, expensive jewelry, fancy cars, etc., would also seem a logical place to raise revenue and lessen the ever-widening spread between the top and bottom of the pyramid. In 1991, a ten percent luxury tax was imposed on the sale of boats over $100,000, cars of $30,000, and furs and jewelry over $10,000. However, even a billionaire does not buy a yacht or other major luxury every year, so relatively little tax revenue was generated with the luxury tax. Moreover, some felt the luxury tax hurt more than it helped. With the added tax, sales of yachts reportedly declined, and with the drop in sales, there was a corresponding drop in employment in the yacht-building industry.

As the luxury tax did not bring the revenue anticipated and possibly cost jobs, the luxury tax was phased out over several years. Still, as a symbolic gesture, a very graduated sales tax on luxury goods should be re-imposed. With a graduated sales tax, an affluent family buying a sailboat or fishing boat for the family would pay a token amount, but a billionaire executive buying a yacht would pay a modest amount, say three percent. A three percent increase in the price of yachts would likely not affect sales or employment. However, a three percent tax on a five million dollar yacht would pay for school lunches for about 45,000 children.

The United States has approximately fifteen million millionaires. Most of these individuals are "paper millionaires," meaning they are millionaires because of the equity in their home, their farm, or a family-owned business. With their assets tied up in equity on a day-to-day basis, these millionaires are merely upper-middle-class. They may go out to eat more often or drive nicer cars than most Americans, but they still shop at Costco, fly coach, and a luxury purchase, like a boat, is for family outings, not for a yacht to sail in the Caribbean. Functionally, paper millionaires are upper-middle-class and are not "rich" in the normal sense of the word.

Dramatically increasing the individual income tax on "paper millionaires" to close the wealth gap would mean paper millionaires would have less discretionary income. They would go out to eat less often, take cheaper vacations, decide against buying a boat for the family, and so on. With less discretionary income being pumped into the economy, layoffs would be inevitable, and that would create more, not less, poverty.

Let's next consider others, like professional athletes and actors, that are not "paper millionaires" but truly earn tens of millions a year. The combined salaries for players in the three major sports (football, basketball, baseball) is about fourteen billion dollars. However, a career in professional sports is usually short-lived, and there is always the chance of permanent injury. Given their short careers and physical risk, taxing wealthy professional athletes to support the poor seems unfair. Further, many professional athletes donate time (and money) to worthy causes to help the underprivileged. If professional athletes had to "give at work," they would be less likely to continue their charitable work.

Actors in big-budget movies can make millions, but the entire US gross revenue for major film companies in a typical year is just over eleven billion or roughly just a little less than the salaries for the players in the three major sports. Moreover, nowadays, much movie production occurs overseas. Taxing highly paid actors would drive even movie production overseas, creating even more unemployment in the US film industry.

But what about those high-paying executives? Those who make more in a week, or even a day, than their typical worker, makes in a year. What about taxing them? First off, as with professional athletes and major movie stars there are not of them. Taking the top ten highest paid executives from every Fortune 5000 company, is only 5,000 people. Moreover, for top executives most of their compensation, comes in the form of stock or stock options (making the rationale for a modest sales tax that much more compelling). As there are so few "mega-earners," even a significant increase in the top tax rate would generate comparatively little tax revenue.

Executive salaries, like ordinary salaries, are normally deductible as corporate business expenses. However, beginning in 2017, only the first million in executive pay is counted as a business expense. (Because of The Affordable Care Act, the limit for medical companies is $500,000). However, the million (or half-million) limit has done little to control the escalating salaries of CEOs and top executives of major corporations, mega-earners that earn more in a day than a file clerk, custodian, or security guard earns in a year.

Rich or poor, parents are supposed to instill values in their children. The children of a CEO that *only* makes a hundred times the average worker will learn a different set of values than the children of a CEO that makes *five hundred* times that of the average worker. Similarly, the children of an ordinary worker that makes only one-hundredth of the salary CEO will have a more favorable view of capitalism than the children of an ordinary worker, where the "big bosses" earn five hundred times as much as their parents.

In 1948, with the urging of the United States, the United Nations adopted the Universal Declaration of Human Rights. The Universal Declaration of Human Rights reads very much like the U.S. Bill of Rights. There are provisions for freedom of religion, the right to life and liberty, the right to a fair trial, and so on. Among the rights is the right to work, to form unions, and that "everyone who works has the right to just and favorable remuneration . . ." When the *average* employee is paid less for a day than the CEO makes in a year, that is not "just and favorable remuneration."

In addition to current provisions of law, to achieve "just and favorable remuneration," companies should be heavily taxed if the ratio of CEO to average worker is excessive. What is excessive? Three hundred sixty-five to one would be a plausible figure. Anything more than "a year for a day" is a failure of America to honor its commitment "that *everyone* who works has the right to just and favorable remuneration." Moreover, compared to other industrial countries, "a day for a year" is still a massive wage gap.

While the rise in CEO compensation has far-outpaced the rise in wages for the average worker, the ever-narrowing apex and ever-widening base of the pyramid is **not** because the top tax rate was slightly lowered or because there is no longer a tax on luxuries, or because the tax on capital gains is slightly lower than its historical norm. The increasing gap between the haves and the haves-not-so has to do with the escalating cost of housing (see appendix for details) and population growth.

The birth rate for households earning $200,000 or more is about two-thirds of the birth rate in households where the income is between $15,000 and $35,000. Increasing the capital gain tax rate, re-imposing a tax on luxury goods, imposing a tax on the sale of stock, penalizing companies that pay excess top executives more for a day's work than a year's wages for the average worker, justified as these actions are, would only marginally compensate for the widening of the base of the pyramid due to population growth and the decline in homeownership.

While the wealth apex is broadening at the base and narrowing at the top, the middle class still holds the majority of wealth. The middle class can be divided into three parts. The upper-middle-class, the middle-middle, and the lower-middle. The upper-middle-class would include "paper millionaires," most professionals (doctors, dentists, lawyers, etc.), and successful local business owners. Persons in the upper-middle usually own their own homes, and when they die, their children inherit the equity in their homes.

Many of the jobs in the middle-middle class, police officer, teacher, bus driver, etc., are in the public or health sector (nurse, lab technician, physical therapist, etc.). Traditionally, those in the middle-middle earned enough to buy a home. However, as the price of housing has outpaced the growth in wages, fewer and fewer of the middle-middle class can afford to buy a home.

Those in the lower-middle class are mostly employed in the private sector. Numerically, this is the largest class, but their wealth is modest. Homeownership is much less common. If someone in this class does own a home, it is a modest one, maybe a mobile home in a nice (or not so nice) mobile home park. Moreover, because of their higher birthrate in this class, when a homeowner in this class dies, there are more heirs to divide the modest equity. Whereas, when affluent homeowners die, there is substantial equity, and, typically, that equity is divided among only one or two children.

The poor can be subdivided into the working poor and the chronically unemployed. The working poor find employment at (or just above) minimum wage. (Forty percent of those working in fast food are over the age of twenty-five). For the working poor, even affording rent on a modest apartment is a challenge. The "lucky ones" have government-financed housing.

The chronically unemployed often become the unhoused. It is estimated twenty-five percent of those without housing have a serious mental health disorder. Further, whether or not they meet the clinical definition of depression or other mental health disorder, unhoused children suffer emotionally, if not physically. The memories of sleeping week after week in a homeless shelter or the family car last a lifetime.

Adults and children that comprise the poorest class are largely dependent on government assistance. Breaking that dependency is labor-intensive and expensive. Preventing poverty in the first place, of course, is a lot cheaper than trying to remedy it.

One way to prevent poverty should be unemployment benefits. As indicated in chapter one, capitalism is much more fluid in the 21st century than in the past. Hard-working Americans that lose their jobs due to corporate restructuring, technological advances, or market forces, or other forces beyond their control deserve a meaningful safety net. However, in many states, outside of pandemic relief, unemployment benefits are a mere four percent of base pay. (In Kentucky, it is just over one percent). With unemployment benefits being just four percent of base pay, unemployment can quickly mean slipping into poverty. The federal government should mandate states pay forty percent of base pay in unemployment benefits. Forty percent *might* be enough to cover rent and utilities and prevent the unemployed from becoming the unhoused.

While providing a safety net for the unemployed is important, the priority should be to get the individual working again. Statistically, every month that goes without a job makes finding a job harder. This is understandable, employers want to hire those whose skills are fresh and are already employed and proving their worth to their current employer. However, it is illegal to discriminate simply because an applicant is unemployed, but proving such discrimination is difficult. To enforce the law, the government *could* hire legions of civil servants to more thoroughly investigate claims of unlawful discrimination against the unemployed.

More effective than a legion of civil servants would be to provide a tax break to hire the unemployed. For instance, if a new hire had been unemployed for four months, the company could get a bonus equal to three months of unemployment benefits. This simple change would prevent the unemployed from slipping into the ranks of the newly poor. Moreover, a tax break helping the unemployed become employed would help the government's bottom line. The government would collect taxes on the wages instead of paying out unemployment and other social benefits. By providing the dignity of work, the private sector would be providing a much-needed public service.

Some in the business community providing would likely label such a program as featherbedding. There would be a kernel of truth to such a label. However, the tax benefits of hiring the unemployed could be capped at three percent of the workforce. If a company needed 1000 employees to make ten million widgets a year, employing 1030 employees to make ten million widgets would cause minimal disruption in work production and only minimally increase costs. However, for those thirty employees – and the children of those employees – it would make a tremendous difference. Poverty would be averted.

If every company that employed more than a thousand workers employed just one percent of the longer-term unemployed, that would be 483,000 employees. Assuming three children per two employees, that it is a million lives changed. A million lives changed *without having to raise taxes* and having a *positive* impact on the bottom line of state and federal government.

The budget for the federal government has often been described as "guns versus butter." An aircraft carrier equals so many vouchers for public housing. A tank, so many school lunches, and so on. While a useful insight, the analogy goes only so far. Every government agency, from the FAA to the FBI, to the National Park Service, has a wish list of things they would do -- only if they had the extra money. The National Parks Services alone has a backlog of over eleven *billion* dollars of deferred maintenance on roads, sewage systems and trails. Similarly, the National Science Foundation approves just over twenty-fiver percent of the research proposals it receives from universities and research institutes. If the National Science Foundation had more money, America -- not another country -- would discover the scientific principles behind the next technological breakthrough.

In addition to the often meager unemployment benefits, the government, in the form of the Earned Income Credit, in a very modest way, helps lower-wage earners from becoming truly poor. With the Earned Income Credit, a married couple without children who had *some* income during the year but earned less than $21,000 can receive a *maximum* credit of $538 on their taxes. Five hundred and three eight dollars is a sizable amount of money for a poor person, but certainly not an amount that will help a young married couple break out of poverty.

If the same married couple has three children, the income limit is just over $56,000, and the Earned Income Credit is $6,600. Sixty-six hundred dollars is enough to buy a used car. A car to take to work instead of the bus, so the earned income credit can make an appreciable difference in people's lives. However, the benefit is not a generous as it seems. As the couple's income approaches the $56,000 limit, their tax obligation increases, so the net benefit is likely less than $6,600. Further, under the Earned Income Credit, there is no minimum of hours needed to meet the work requirement. So a woman (or man) working a week at the local McDonald's is entitled to more assistance than if she (or he) worked the entire school year as a cafeteria worker.

The Earned Income Credit program costs the federal government about fifty-six billion dollars. The cost for the Earned Income Credit is roughly *double* the budgets of the National Science Foundation, the National Park Service, the FBI, and the FAA *combined*.

Even with the Earned Income Credit and social welfare programs, thirty-eight million Americans live below the poverty level. Sixty-six million Americans are poor enough to qualify for free health care through Medicaid. Also, recall that nearly two-thirds of all children are born into families poor enough to qualify for WIC. For the sake of simplicity's sake, let's say there are seventy-five million Americans who live in poverty or just one or two small notches above. Seventy-five million Americans that are at least partially dependent on government-funded support. However, before considering how to reduce that seventy-five million we need to consider how the workplace has changed since 1960s and how it is expected to change in the future.

CHAPTER SEVEN

THE CHANGING WORKFORCE, MARKET FORCES, AND WELFARE REFORM

In the 1960s, when the War on Poverty was begun, few could foresee the adverse effects of technological progress or the changing role of women in the workforce. A popular cartoon of the era, *The Jetsons*, reflected this. At work, George Jetson could put his feet up on his desk and let machines do the actual work. At home, his wife, Jane, had a robotic maid named Rosie for household chores and help raise the children. Life in the future was easy -- even the family dog had a high-tech treadmill to use with George.

In the 1960s, container ships were just beginning to replace traditional cargo ships. Unloading cargo from traditional cargo ships was labor-intensive and required an (all-male) crew of longshoremen. However, when cargo is transported by a container ship, a single crane operator can unload an entire ship's cargo in a matter of hours. In 1980 general cargo ships still outnumbered container ships ten to one. However, in the early 21st century, almost all general cargo is transported by container ship. Now, a longshoreman can be a man or a woman, but is still usually a man. They make good money; some longshoremen make over $90,000 a year.

Most of America's consumer goods come from China and other Asian countries. These consumer goods are offloaded on West Coast ports by longshoremen. Unloading those billions and billions of dollars of cargo takes only about 36,000 longshoremen. Container ships have helped international trade, but if cargo still needed to be unloaded by a large crew, there would be many more good-paying jobs for men and women.

Work as a miner, like work as a longshoreman, was once an all-male vocation, as women, by law, were prohibited form working in dangerous jobs such as mining. In 1923, 883,000 men were employed as coal miners. Today employment in the mining industry is still ninety-two percent male, and only a third of the women employed in the coal industry are actual miners. (The rest are engineers, management, lawyers, and clerical staff).

Because of technological advances, environmental concerns, and market forces, there are now only 50,000 coal miners. Adjusted for the rise in population since 1923, that is the equivalent of 23,000 jobs. So today, the chance of a man having a good-paying job as a coal miner is about *three-hundredths* of what it was in 1923.

Similarly, in the past, a woman could have a decent paying job as a telephone operator (ninety-eight percent of telephone operators are women). In the 1940s, there were over 350,000 telephone operators. In 2019, there were just over 4,000.

Now, as in the past, garbage collectors remain a nearly all-male vocation. Only about one percent of "garbage men" are women. Beginning in the 1960s, garbage trucks began having side loaders. The garbage man no longer had to heave a heavy bin into a truck; a mechanical arm did the lifting. With a mechanical arm doing the lifting, it took less time for garbage men to complete their routes, thus reducing the demand for garbage workers. However, the efficiency of employing a side loader has been more than offset by the increase in population. From 1980 to 2020, the population of the United States increased by almost fifty percent (226 million to 330 million). As long as the population increases, the demand for garbage workers will increase.

Another previously male-dominated occupation, and an occupation that has not been subject to technological change, is that of bus driver. Driving a bus in 2020 isn't that much different than diving a bus in 1965. In 1965, almost all bus drivers were men. Now, according to the Bureau of Labor Statistics (BLS), women make up nearly half of the over 500,000 bus drivers.

Two other, once exclusively male occupations, law enforcement, and firefighters, are still fundamentally the same. Squad cars may have computers, and officers may carry Tasers, but police officers still patrol streets, issue tickets, and handcuff suspects, as they did in 1965. Firefighters' equipment has improved, but, as in 1965, firefighters still hook up hoses to fire hydrants to fight fires. Now about twelve percent of sworn law enforcement officers and four percent of all firefighters are women. Today, as in 1965, women are the majority of emergency dispatchers.

As in the private sector, men in the public sector hold the majority of top jobs. However, in the public sector, top jobs are usually appointed by a governor or a President. When a new governor or President is elected, there is a new slate of appointees, so top jobs in the public sector have a built-in instability factor. One major exemption is that of a judge, federal judges are appointed for life, and state judges rarely lose their jobs, so judicial vacancies are rare.

In his first year in office, Governor Newsom of California made sixteen judicial appointments, and eleven were for women. At the federal level, President Trump nominated 177 judges, and about twenty-three percent were women. (Nine out of eleven of Biden's first judicial appointments were women). As women now outnumber men in law schools by nearly two to one, the pool of men available to appoint to become a judge will eventually shrink. However, because of the extraordinary job security judges enjoy, at least for the next few decades, men will remain the majority of judges.

For each top job, like a judge or department head, there are dozens, if not hundreds, employed in lesser public sector jobs. Jobs that are predominately held by women. Want to file for divorce or get a copy of a police report? The file clerk is most likely to be a woman. Have a court case? The court stenographer is almost assuredly a woman. Want to apply for welfare? Your caseworker is very likely to be a woman. What to check out a book from the public library, eighty-three percent of librarians are women. Need "manpower" in a pandemic? Almost all public health nurses are women.

Need to report your child is sick from school? The school secretary is almost assuredly a woman. Want to meet with your child's principal? A school principal is now more likely to be a woman than a man. Want to talk with your child's guidance counselor? Female guidance counselors now outnumber male guidance counselors by a margin of seven to three. Want to talk with your child's teacher? Of the three and a half million public school teachers, three-quarters are women (and that percentage is increasing) and teachers with tenure enjoy an extra level of job protection. Simply put, especially at the local government level, most non-law enforcement occupations in the public sector are predominately held by women. They enjoy job security not available to men or women in the private sector.

However, public sector jobs are not immune from automation. Automation has rendered the public sector occupation of toll-booth attendant (a job with no educational requirements) almost nonexistent. Other routine tax and fine collections, like registering a car or paying a parking fine, can be done online. Instead of a file clerk (who most likely was a woman) processing a payment, a taxpayer inputs data in the format needed, and a computer does the rest. Essentially, the labor involved in registering a car or paying a parking ticket has been outsourced to the individual. Similarly, the private sector has outsourced tasks to the consumer. In the pre-internet days, to place an order, a customer completed and mailed in an order form or called a customer service representative; either way, human hands processed the order, human hands that most likely belonged to a woman.

Similarly, online shopping has cut heavily into the need for cashiers (seventy-two percent of cashiers are women). Many retailers, especially stores like Macy's, J.C. Penney's, Sears, and The Gap, where clothing constituted all or a large portion of sales, declared bankruptcy. In past years, a woman who worked as a cashier at a retail store could expect a promotion to supervisor after so many years of loyal service now has no job at all.

Of course, the decline in retail sales meant an increase in online sales. Warehouses of products need warehouse workers, and about two-thirds of warehouse workers are men. Industrial robots, however, are increasingly automating the process of stocking and shipping. More industrial robots stocking shelves and shipping orders will mean fewer jobs, jobs predominately held by men. At the retail level, cashiers often do double duty as stocking clerks, but industrial robots in retail stores, unlike in large warehouses, is many decades away.

Of course, before a product can be shipped, it needs to be manufactured. Manufacturing is a largely male-dominated job. From 1970 to 2016, the percentage of men employed in manufacturing varied from a high of 71.4 to a low of 66.4 percent. In 2019, just under thirteen million men and women were employed in manufacturing, and 2019 was slightly better than the previous few years. However, in 1980 nineteen and half million Americans were employed in manufacturing. From 1980 to 2019, America's population grew by a hundred million. Millions more need work, but there are only about two-thirds the number of good-paying factory jobs as before.

While the decline in manufacturing affected men more than women, in one sub-category, apparel manufacture, almost exclusively women, suffered. In 1990 over 900,000, were employed as garment workers. In 2019, it was just over 100,000.

Unlike a woman in the past who might have earned a decent salary as a telephone operator or as a union-member garment worker, today, a woman working today as a cashier, like male cashiers, is paid minimum wage or just above. Yet, technological progress threatens even the job of cashier. Many major retailers, like Walmart and Target, now have self-checkout lines. McDonald's, Taco Bell, and other fast-food restaurants also have self-ordering counters. However, major retailers, and fast-food chains like McDonald's and Taco Bell, are *almost always* hiring for their minimum wage jobs. The self-pay stations at major retailers or fast food chains are more the result of a *labor shortage* for minimum wage jobs than a cost-saving measure.

The same is *not true* for self-pay stations in traditional supermarkets. Self-pay stations in traditional supermarkets save employers money. Workers in traditional supermarkets are usually represented by a union. A cashier at a major supermarket who belongs to a union with five years' experience earns about $18/hour. However, food sales in non-union retail businesses like Walmart and Target, stores with self-pay stations, have cut heavily into food sales at traditional supermarkets. Nonunion Wal-Mart now sells more food than the two largest supermarket chains (Kroger and Albertsons) combined.

Go into any bank, and, as with cashiers, the teller is most likely to be a woman (eighty percent of all tellers are women). Automatic teller machines (ATMs) started to become commonplace in the 1980s. However, consumer habits change slowly, and the number of tellers remained steady at about 500,000 for several years. At the beginning of the 21St Century, the number of tellers began to decline, and in 2015 their numbers began to rapidly decline. The advent of ATMs was not the only reason for the decline. With the increase of online and mobile banking, many banks consolidated branches. Government projections say there will be 414,000 tellers in 2028, so in 2028 approximately 68,000 women who might have been steadily employed as tellers will need to find other work.

In the COVID pandemic, the travel industry was hit especially hard. Tens of thousands of women working as flight attendants, or airline customer representatives, lost their jobs. (Roughly two-thirds of all flight attendants and customer service representatives are women).

Tens of thousands of men in the travel industry also lost "honest jobs" jobs. Honest jobs as baggage handlers or aircraft mechanics (ninety-five percent of mechanics are men, and almost all baggage handlers are men). Aircraft mechanics need specialized training, but a high school diploma isn't required to be a good baggage handler. However, a high school diploma, at least, is need needed to be a flight attendant or a customer service representative.

Thousands of pilots were laid off in the pandemic, and ninety-five percent of pilots are men. While not required by the FAA, major airlines require pilots to have a college degree. Also, almost all scheduled flights are now flown by just a pilot and co-pilot, technological progress making the occupation of flight engineer (previously called a navigator) obsolete.

As the airline industry rebounds from the pandemic, it will be mostly men who will return to the good-paying occupations of pilot and mechanic. However, unlike in generations where a man (in past generations, it was almost always a man) obtained pilot or mechanical training in the military, the majority of pilots and mechanics now obtain training at their own expense. To be an aircraft mechanic can cost over $20,000; to become a pilot can cost over $80,000.

Prior to the pandemic, the airline industry was growing faster than the overall economy. Job growth means greater job security. When the effects of the pandemic are a thing of the past, demand will increase for good-paying jobs like pilot or mechanic but also for more mundane jobs like baggage handler and customer service representative.

As the pandemic recedes, employment in travel-related jobs, like hotel housekeepers (ninety-five percent female) and desk clerks (sixty percent male), will increase. However, even after the travel industry fully rebounds from the pandemic, there will still be very few travel agents (eighty percent of travel agents are women). Technological progress has allowed customers to make their own travel arrangements rendering the occupation of travel agent nearly extinct.

The pandemic also hit the restaurant industry very hard. Ten of thousands of waiters, waitresses, and dishwashers lost their jobs. Seventy percent of restaurant servers are women, and eighty percent of dishwashers are men. There are no educational requirements to be a dishwasher or waiter/waitress. A server at a five-star restaurant can earn upwards of $80,000 a year. Head chefs at (who are most often men) five-star restaurants can earn over $100,000. However, a dishwasher at a five-star restaurant isn't paid much more than a dishwasher at an IHOP or Denny's. Likewise, line cooks at a five-star restaurant (who most often are men) make much less than those who serve the food (who, as noted, are usually women).

While the travel and restaurant industry will recover from the pandemic, jobs like telephone operator or garment worker are never coming back. Similarly, both because of technological progress and market forces, the demand for coal miners, general factory workers, tellers, travel agents, and many other honest decent-paying jobs, jobs that do not require education beyond high school will remain scarce.

In past generations, a man (or occasionally a woman) with no more a high school education and a good driving record could get a job as a cab driver. As a cab driver, he (or she) could earn an honest, if modest, wage. However, ride-sharing services have cut deeply into the incomes of cab drivers. Nearly two-thirds of cab drivers are nearly two-thirds of the drivers for ride-sharing companies are men. Experts generally agree that driverless cars will be a reality in the not-too-distant future. Uber has already test-piloted driverless vehicles. Domino's pizza is testing driverless pizza delivery. Such automation will hurt the job prospects for men more than for women.

Jobs in the health care industry are largely immune from market forces. In good times and bad, people still get sick. Further, as the population ages, nursing homes need more health care aides, housekeepers, and skilled medical staff. With its low birth rate and long life expectancy, the shortage of home health aides is particularly acute in Japan. Japan has invested billions of yen in developing robots for the nursing home market. Some elderly in Japan's nursing homes can enjoy simple interactions with a robot, robotic companionship being better than no companionship at all. However, full-service robots, like Rosie, that can make beds or do laundry remain the stuff of science-fiction.

Skilled medical jobs, jobs that require specialized training but not a four-year college degree, are largely insulated from automation or overseas competition. These jobs are primarily held by women. Ninety-five percent of dental hygienists are women. Eighty-four percent of lab technicians are women, seventy-eighty percent of x-ray technicians, and seventy-three percent of respiratory therapists are women. Like aircraft mechanics and pilots, those looking to be employed as dental hygienists, x-ray technicians, etc., pay for their pre-employment training, often through a low-cost community college.

In the private sector, for non-health-related jobs, job security varies considerably. Some private-sector jobs have considerable job security and are protected from low-cost overseas labor or automation. For instance, except in a pandemic, hairstylists and barbers are always needed to cut hair. Barbers and hairstylists, like skilled health professions, have to complete a training program and pass certification exams, but the cost for such training is relatively minimal. In previous generations, men got their hair cut at a barbershop by a man, and women got their haircut at a beauty parlor by a woman. However, market forces have forced many beauty parlors and most traditional barbershops out of business. Now, unisex chains like *Supercuts* or *Fantastic Sam's* are where most men (and some women) get their hair cut, and staff at unisex chains are almost exclusively women.

A male-dominated private-sector job protected from low-cost overseas labor and automation is that of the skilled construction worker (eighty-eight percent of construction workers are men). However, like employment in the travel industry, employment in construction is highly dependent on the economy. In a recession, even the best skilled, hardest-working, most-experienced construction worker will find it hard to find work. Construction is also dependent on the weather. When there is rain or snow, there is no work, and no work means no paycheck.

Further, for a given area, new construction, whether residential or commercial, hits a saturation level. Whether to build a house, office building, or factory, on-site construction is a one-time need, while health care and haircuts are ongoing needs. Moreover, few construction workers who are fifty-five years old can "pound nails" like they could when they were twenty-five, while, at fifty-five, a nurse, teacher, lab technician, stenographer, librarian, hairstylist, etc., can be as capable as she has ever been.

The skilled on-site construction worker, however, is not fully protected from the threat of automation. As more and more Americans cannot afford traditional homes, the demand for manufactured homes (aka mobile homes) has increased thirty percent from 2015 to 2019. In a factory, as opposed to a job site, automation is possible. Also, as a side note, the owner of a manufactured home usually has to pay rent on the space that the mobile home occupies. Sometimes space rent can exceed that of the mortgage payment, making homeowners of mobile homes more renters than owners. Also, the useful lifespan of a manufactured home is much less than that of a traditional home, so heirs have less equity to inherit.

Technological progress, of course, has created jobs that did not exist in previous generations. In the 1960s, cable TV was in its infancy. There were only a handful of "cable guys" (and virtually all were men). A cable installer is still most likely to be a man. A cable installer, like a flight attendant, does not require any formal education beyond high school. The Bureau of Labor Statistics projects zero job growth for cable installers.

In the 1960s, there was no internet, and computers were housed in specially air-conditioned rooms. In the 1960s, only a handful of colleges offered degrees in computer sciences; now, a major in computer science is commonplace. The gender gap is closing; still, many more men major in computer science and related majors than women.

Today, as in the sixties, a young person graduating with a degree in computer science or a similar field is almost assured of employment after graduation. However, much like the construction worker, information technology is a young person's game. The average age of an employee at Google is just thirty. Other companies like Apple, Microsoft, and, Adobe have a similar tilt toward the younger generation, making a man or woman's career in big tech likely short-lived.

As in the past, an individual with a college earns significantly more during their lifetime than someone without a degree. Women now outnumber men in college; for every eight men in college, there are eleven women. Already, sixty percent of the doctors under the age of thirty-five are women. Further, roughly two-thirds of all students studying to be optometrists, pharmacists, psychologists, attorneys, and a whopping seventy percent of veterinarian students are women. By the mid-century, the majority of Americans with college degrees will be women, and women will be a decided majority of doctors, lawyers, optometrists, pharmacists, psychologists, and veterinarians.

If a professional woman and her husband divorce, and the father becomes remiss in his child support, the professional woman still has significant income. If a woman has a secure skilled job, such as in the public sector or the health industry, and the father becomes remiss in child support, it might be difficult, but with a middle-class, secure job, she can "make do."

However, if she has a modest paying job and the father of children becomes remiss in his child support, her situation becomes dire. She might not be able to afford to put gas in or pay for a much-needed repair for her older-model car and have to the bus to work. (Incidentally, inexpensive older model cars are less fuel-inefficient than newer cars. This makes a gas tax a greater burden on the poor). To get by, a woman with children employed in an honest but low-paying job who doesn't receive child support is in a real bind. She doesn't earn anywhere near enough to pay for rent, child care, and groceries. She may have to go on welfare.

On welfare, she hopes her caseworker can help her get government-funded housing or at least government-funded child care. If she has child care, she can work, and her earnings can supplement her welfare grant. (In a complicated formula that varies by state, a recipient on welfare, up to a certain limit, is not penalized for earning a paycheck. Once that limit is reached, the welfare grant is gradually reduced as earnings increase).

Out-of-home fathers whose children are on welfare, generally have little or no education beyond high school. Compared to the past, his ability to find an "honest" decent-paying job like a factory worker is greatly diminished. If he takes a job as a dishwasher or other low-paying job, after child support is collected, he lives well below the poverty level.

If, through a job training program or some other path, the mother finds a better-paying job and gets off welfare, the father's child support will continue to go to the government (less fifty dollars in some states) until the father's back child support is recovered. If the father was significantly in arrears, it can take months for the child support to begin flowing to the mother once she is off welfare. In the meantime, the children suffer. They do not get the benefit of their father's child support.

Rich or poor, when a couple with children separates, the woman will likely want a new man in her life, and the man will likely want a new woman in his life (if they haven't already found a new partner). For a single woman on welfare, the pool of "good men" available is quite small. Few men with good-paying jobs are interested in a woman with children on welfare. For the woman on welfare, even if he is "good" to her and her children, her new man is likely to be unemployed or marginally employed.

She and her new man may have a committed relationship, or it may be a more casual arrangement. From your author's thirty-four years' experience in social services, the casual arrangement is far more common. Whatever the level of commitment, she and her new man, intentionally or unintentionally, may have a child, and another child is added to that seventy-five million denominator.

To discourage adding another child to the seventy-five million denominator California and many other states tried denying additional benefits for the additional child. As the child was likely the product of a "casual commitment," denying benefits seemed morally justified; there was no reason to incentivize illegitimate births.

Denying welfare benefits for the additional child also appealed to a notion of economic responsibility. It just wasn't fair for the taxpayer to foot the bill for *another child*. By way of analogy, most states have mandatory helmet laws for motorcycle riders. If the motorcycle rider gets into an accident and doesn't have a helmet, the cost to treat the rider's injuries can be much greater. If the rider had government-funded medical insurance, the riders' failure to wear a helmet is an additional cost to the taxpayer. Similarly, a welfare mother should be expected to exercise responsibility and not have another child causing an additional burden to the taxpayer.

However, "the no additional benefits for the additional child" rule was not economically prudent. If a woman on welfare with two children has a third child she struggles even more if her grant remains calculate for a family of three. Her "income" is woefully inadequate for even basic needs. She is focused not just making it through the month, but through the week, even the day. The chances that she and her children will break of poverty are close to nil. The policy of denying benefits for the additional child caused children to suffer and was a greater cost to the taxpayer.

Of course, even with the threat that there would be no additional aid for an additional child, some women had another child. (Many, no doubt, that were unplanned). One woman in your author's caseload, we will call her Rosalie, had four children. Rosalie received aid as a family of three (herself and her two children). As a household of five but only with an income intended for three, the children suffered. Largely, but not exclusively, attributable to Rosalie's extreme poverty, the children suffered. Based on neglect, I asked a judge to sign a warrant to remove the children from Rosalie's care. The judge signed the warrant, and the children were placed in foster care. Without her welfare check, Rosalie lost her very modest apartment and became one of the homeless.

As required by law, there were several court hearings, but Rosalie was never able to get her children returned to her care, and her children remained in foster care. Over several years, the state paid tens of thousands of dollars in foster care and adoption assistance payments.

California and other states have since discontinued the practice of denying additional benefits for the additional child. A handful of states continue to do so. Both on moral and economic grounds, federal regulations need to ban the practice nationwide.

If a woman is sufficiently poor to qualify for medical care, under the Affordable Care Act, she can get free contraceptive medical care. However, if she is not "in love" with someone when she sees her health care provider, she may see no reason to be on birth control. If she is otherwise healthy, her next medical appointment might not be for a year. During the year, before she becomes sexually active again, she *may* have the wisdom to be responsible and start birth control. However, like an affluent woman, a poor woman can get carried away in the moment and risk pregnancy if her new man fails to come prepared for a romantic encounter.

An APA-style should be conducted on the cost-benefit ratio of mailing condoms to women on welfare. Would this lead to a reduction in the number of pregnancies? Would it reduce public health costs for the treatment of STDs? Such a study would be relatively inexpensive but potentially could lead to new policies that could save millions, if not billions, of dollars. But why stop at welfare moms? Why not the absent father? Why not, in welfare cases, send absent fathers condoms as well? Except for the collection of child support, the welfare system largely ignores the absent father. As he is likely unemployed or marginally employed, he likely qualifies for government-funded health care as well. The absent father needs job training just as much as the mom on welfare.

In a strong majority of the households on welfare, the biological father is not in the home. Sometimes the mother has no idea where the father is living. Other times because he is incarcerated, the mother knows exactly where the father is living. Other times, as we saw with the stories of Anna and Tonya in chapter five, simply because the father does not have a stable income, the father does not have a stable address. Other times, the mother does not know where the father because she simply doesn't know who the father is. Over my career, your author has had dozens of cases where the identity of the father was unknown.

Also, to state the obvious, one man can impregnate multiple women. One such man was "Jim." Jim was a drifter with no job skills and no steady job. However, in a short span of time, by three different women, Jim fathered three children. In separate child welfare cases, all three children were removed from their respective mothers' care and placed in foster care. None of the children were placed with Jim. Jim was unable to lawfully support himself, to say nothing of supporting a child.

Jim was just one father in one child welfare case, but because of his causal procreation, the taxpayer had to support his children in foster care. In the larger welfare system, there are undoubtedly many "Jims." Jims who father children they are unable to support. Jims who do not have job skills. Jims who did not or barely graduated high school. Jims who engage in criminal conduct either to support themselves or simply to give their life focus, albeit an illegal one.

What can the government do to discourage poor men (like Jim) and poor women (like Rosalie) from adding to that seventy-five million denominator of the poor? The answer is to expand the Earned Income Credit to young, poor adults *before* they have children. If an individual is poor *and* childless, there should be a financial incentive for them to remain childless. Giving a tax to credit to the poor for deferring having a child would be far cheaper than having government (aka taxpayers) support another child in poverty. The cost of medical care, cash aid, food stamps, school lunches, etc., from birth through age eighteen for a child in poverty is in the range of $200,000. There are savings to be had. The tax credit for not having a child, while poor, could be substantial and still be cost-effective.

Of course, a tax credit for the poor to remain childless needs a cut-off age. It would be a waste of tax dollars to provide a financial incentive to poor women beyond their child-bearing years not to bear a child (or for poor older men, whose likelihood of fathering a child is close to nil already). Is there a rational cut-off age? There is. The prefrontal cortex, the part of the brain where impulse controls develops, is not fully-formed until age twenty-five.

Men, specifically young men, are responsible for the majority of crime. The vast majority of criminal behavior is opportunistic, a product of poor impulse control. Crimes committed with minimal forethought and little consideration of the possible consequences, crimes that *might not have occurred* if the prefrontal cortex had been fully functioning. A tax credit for a young poor adult to remain childless and law abiding would reduce crime and welfare caseloads. Given the high cost of incarceration, judicial system costs, the medical cost to treat victims of violent crime, rewarding lawful behavior for poor men not to father a child, and poor women for not getting pregnant would be more cost-effective than the current system focused on punishment.

Providing a financial incentive to discourage criminal behavior has another benefit. A man (or woman) with a criminal record has a hard time finding any job at all, to say nothing of a job that provides economic self-sufficiency. In previous generations, a man (or a woman) with a criminal past could hide their past, but not anymore. Today, employers, even employers hiring for lower-paying positions, routinely conduct criminal records for job applicants. In the 21st century, there is no escaping a criminal past. A man (or a woman) with a criminal record can remain unemployed or marginally employed for years. They – and their children --- remain dependent on government assistance. Providing a financial incentive for men and women living in poverty to be law-abiding and remain childless until age twenty-five is a win-win.

Further, if poor men and poor women are incentivized not to have a child until the prefrontal cortex is fully formed when they do become parents, they will be more mature in their child-rearing. With a financial incentive to remain childless while poor, there would be less child abuse and neglect. Moreover, a young, poor woman without children can more easily leave her abusive man than if she has a child. Economically and morally, a tax credit, contingent on lawful behavior, for young, poor adults to remain childless is the right thing to do.

How would such a system work? Wouldn't some enormous government bureaucracy be needed? Not really, criminal records are computerized, welfare rolls are computerized. Payroll records are computerized. Unemployment benefits are computerized. Running computer matches among various government databases would be far cheaper than the in-person interviews and the tedious amounts of paperwork needed for public assistance programs.

But what would happen if a poor woman, under the age of twenty-five, on welfare, had a child? Naturally, she would be ineligible for any more payments. Further, any amounts she had received for not having a child would be deducted from any future tax refund she might receive. The government already intercepts tax refund checks for men (and women) who owe back child support; the same could be done for mothers that received a tax credit to remain childless but had a child anyway. So that's the mother, what about the father?

In the past, when a child was born, whatever name the mother gave to a medical clerk for the father was the name listed on the birth certificate. As social mores have changed and "casual commitment" has become commonplace, paternity laws have changed. Now, if the parents are not married, most states require the father to give his permission before being listed on the birth certificate. With paternity established, if a poor man under twenty-five fathers a child, he, like the mother, would be denied receiving any additional money and subject to a tax intercept for previous payments paid to him for not fathering a child.

Some may object and say, "You can't tell people how to live their lives!" However, social policy is all about discouraging undesired behavior and rewarding desired behavior. The government fines motorcycle riders for not wearing helmets. The government levies fines for driving while using a cell phone. The government taxes cigarettes to discourage smoking. Quite simply, one of the roles of government is to discourage behavior that can harm others, even if that harm is merely an added tax burden to other taxpayers.

However, as the poor have no money, the financial "sticks" of fines would not work. "Carrots" are needed. If the current $56 billion Earned Income Credit is meant to encourage the poor to find work, then surely then a financial incentive to put money into the pockets of the poor to the young poor to remain childless makes equal sense. Such incentives would reduce the need to raise taxes or increase debt to pay for social welfare programs.

CHAPTER EIGHT

THE THREE-LEGGED STOOL MEETS THE 21ST CENTURY

A young adult living in poverty with a good work ethic, some government assistance, and a dose of luck *might* break out of poverty and land a Horatio Alger job or, if extremely driven, exceptionally talented, and extraordinarily lucky, move into the upper economic stratum. However, an elderly person living in poverty will almost assuredly die in poverty.

In 1935, when the social security program began, social security was described as one leg of a three-legged stool. The other two legs of the "stool" being private savings and pensions. Today, according to the Social Security Administration, forty-five percent of all unmarried recipients and twenty-one percent of married recipients rely on social security for ninety percent or more of their income. Also, as noted in chapter one, about nine percent of retirees are poor enough to qualify for food stamps.

The average social security check is just over $1500/month. If a husband and wife each receive an average check, their annual income is a modest, if livable, $36,000. If, as is typical, the husband dies first and the wife earned less than her husband, she receives a supplement to her social security so that her monthly benefit is equal to her late husband's. If her late husband earned an average income after his death, she receives $17,580 a year, an amount just about the poverty level.

The monthly benefit for someone was earning $45,000 is more half than for someone that earned $90,000 a year, so social security favors lower wage earners. Further, social security taxes are only imposed on the first $137,700 of earnings, so it is the moderately affluent and the rich (up to a point) that subsidize Social Security benefits for lower-wage earners.

The trustees of the social security program issue an annual report regarding the solvency of the social security system. Consistently the trustees have reported that social security will begin operating at a deficit around the year 2035. If social security taxes were imposed on the first $500,000 instead of the $137,000, that would help keep social security solvent. However, if fewer people of modest means took a disproportional larger share of Social Security dollars, then Social Security would remain solvent even longer.

The pension leg of the three-legged stool comes in two basic types, defined contribution, and defined benefit. Under a defined benefit plan, a retiree, based on their salary and years of service, receives a set amount each month. In 1987, forty million Americans private and public sector employees were enrolled in a defined benefit plan. In 2017, the figure was just over fourteen million – almost all in the public sector. Incidentally, contrary to popular belief, public employees help fund their pensions. The amounts government employees contribute and the benefits they receive as retirees vary greatly. For firefighters and police officers, and others in high-risk jobs, their contributions towards retirement can be ten percent or more of base pay.

In 1974, congress passed the Employee Retirement Insurance Security Act (ERISA). Before ERISA, private pensions were largely unregulated. To meet some real or imagined need, with little more than a promise to pay the money back, a company could raid its retirement fund. With ERISA, managers of a private pension fund have a fiduciary duty to the retirement fund – not the corporation sponsoring the fund. As the pension fund was now obligated to serve the needs of employees/retirees, not the corporation, there was less motivation for corporations to sponsor a defined benefit retirement plan.

Private-sector defined-benefit pension plans also made mergers difficult. When companies merge, the newly combined company assumes the assets and liabilities of the old companies. If Company A has a pension plan wants to merge with Company B, the newly formed company has a legal obligation to fund Company's A pension plan prior to the merger. The financial obligation of Company A's pension plan can make an otherwise desirable merger much less tenable. Moreover, a merger between a company with a pension plan and a company without a pension plan creates two classes of employees, creating built-in friction in the workplace.

As companies shed their pension plans, mergers became more and more attractive. In 1985, the dollar value of mergers was $305 billion per year. In the first decade of the 21st Century, the value of mergers climbed to over $500 billion per year. With so many mergers, there was a corresponding decrease in job security.

Three years after ERISA, congress gave special tax status to a defined contribution retirement plan commonly referred to as a 401 (k) plan. With a 401 (k) plan, a company does not have the financial liability it would have under a defined contribution plan. Also, unlike defined benefit plans, companies offering 401 (k) plans are not required to contribute to their employee's retirement. (Up to a certain percentage, many employers do match their employee's contributions).

Under a company-sponsored 401 (k) plan, an employee can, tax-free, contribute to a personal retirement fund. More than fifty-eight million Americans, the vast majority who hold ordinary jobs, have money in a 401 (k). Contributions to 401 (k) are normally invested in one or more of several mutual stock funds approved by the financial services company the employer has selected.

Of course, the stock market goes up and down. If contributions are made when stock prices are low, the employee owns more shares for each dollar invested. If around an employee's retirement, the stock market goes up, the employee has done particularly well. However, if contributions are made when stock prices are high but at retirement, the stock market goes down, the retiree has relatively less. Thus, because of the vagaries of the stock market, under a defined contribution plan, it is possible for an employee retiring after thirty years of service could have less money than one who retires after twenty-five years of service.

The defined benefit plans of the past were more equitable than the 401 (k) plans of the present.

Of course, for lower-paid employees, saving for retirement is harder than for higher-paid employees. Let's take the example of a single mom with a lower-paying job. Some years she gets child support from the father and makes voluntary contributions to her 401 (k). Other years, when she gets little or no child support, she doesn't contribute to her 401 (k). Let's say over a twenty-year career, half of her years are lean years, and half are good years. In good years she contributes three percent of her $40,000 salary, and her employer matches her three percent. After twenty years of service and ten years of contributions, she has $24,000.

However, let's now consider if she is a higher-earning employee and contributes $3,000 every year for twenty years. If the stock market remains unchanged and with a three percent match from her employer, she has $120,000. However, the stock market will not remain unchanged. Some years will be bad, and some years will be good. If she invests $6,000 a year (her three thousand plus her employer's match) in a stock or mutual fund that normally sells for a hundred dollars by is selling at eighty dollars, she will have purchased seventy-five shares.

If she is issued a dividend of a dollar a share, and the dividend is reinvested (which is customary), she will have 82.5 shares. When the stock returns to the normal price of one hundred dollars a share, she will have $8,250. Over time, buying shares over a set number of years below market is more of a gain than the loss of buying the same set number of shares above market, and the discrepancy increases with the size of the dividend and the length of time. Thus, those who are affluent and contribute to their 401 (k) every year will, on average, earn more than double those who can only afford to contribute every other year.

If, when the employee is first hired and the market is high, they will buy fewer shares in their first year of employment than a new hire when the market is low. Over a lifetime of working, this initial discrepancy can translate into a meaningful difference in assets when the employee retires. Again, a defined contribution plan has a built-in inequity not found in the defined benefit plan.

The tax benefits of a 401 (k) plan are of greater benefit to the higher-earning employee than a lower-earning employee. An individual with a taxable income of $30,000 that makes a $1,000 contribution to a 401 (k) reduces their tax by about $120. An individual with a taxable income of $60,000 making a $1,000 contribution saves $220 on taxes or nearly twice the amount for the same contribution.

In 1975, congress authorized Individual Retirement Accounts (IRAs). A traditional IRA offers much the same benefits as a 401 (k) plan, except there is no "middleman" in the form of a company-sponsored plan; the individual employee, perhaps with professional advice, chooses where to invest for retirement. Like with the 401 (k) plans, no taxes are collected until a withdrawal is made. Presumably, withdrawals will occur in retirement and with reduced income in retirement, withdrawals are taxed a lower rate. The particularly affluent can contribute to a 401 (k), a traditional IRA, and a Roth IRA, where taxes are paid upfront.

Those working in better-paying jobs are better educated. They more easily understand the "fine print" of a 401 plan or an IRA and so can make more informed decisions about how to invest their money. However, millions of Americans know they do not understand the stock market -- except that they know they could lose money. So they put their money away into something they understand --- a savings account at a government-insured bank.

Struggling as they are, less-affluent Americans aren't saving much for retirement. The median (50th percentile) balance in an individual savings account is a modest is seven thousand dollars. Further, unlike a 401 (k) or IRA, where taxes are paid upon withdrawals, interest on a savings account is taxed as it accrues. Therefore, poorer employees are taxed in their working years, while the affluent are taxed in their retirement years. It wouldn't make much difference in practical terms, but to give those of modest means a break available to the more affluent, the first fifty dollars in interest in individual saving accounts should be tax-free.

In generations past, employees could count on their employer providing a Christmas (or more generically, an annual) bonus. While top and some sales executives still receive annual bonuses, company-wide annual (aka holiday) bonuses have all but disappeared. For millions of Americans, tax federal and state refunds are, in essence, their annual bonus. When tax time came around, the parents in my caseload let me know how desperately they needed their tax refund. With the tax refund, they could buy some badly-needed tires for their car or other neglected maintenance. Other times, they needed the tax refund to pay back a relative, friend, sometimes even a boss, from whom they borrowed.

A tax refund is essentially a loan to the government. If a taxpayer has overpaid taxes during the year, the government has use of the excess money until the taxpayer is issued a refund. With a federal tax return, the taxpayer gets that excess back. However, with a state tax refund, instead of the taxpayer getting interest on this "loan" to the state government, the federal government taxes it. Thus, the poor person who borrowed money from a friend or relative and used a tax refund to pay the money back pays interest, not to the friend or relative but to the federal government.

Even more outrageous than taxing state refunds is taxing unemployment benefits. Trying to live on unemployment benefits can mean tapping into savings, savings that might have been earmarked for retirement. At three percent interest, a thousand dollar withdrawal at age thirty means $2,800 less for retirement at age sixty-five.

Moreover, getting a few months behind in bills because of a stretch of unemployment means a drastically lower credit score. Reclaiming a good credit score can take years to reestablish. A poor credit score can make making a large purchase like a home more expensive, if not impossible. Taxing unemployment benefits, meager as they are, is the government's equivalent of putting a dollar in a street musician's hat and taking back a quarter. Simply put, unemployment benefits should not be taxed.

Some feel that individuals on unemployment try to "game the system" and collect unemployment benefits to avoid having to work. However, what is "gaming the system" to one person is sound financial decision-making for another. Early in my career, I met with a woman we will call Norma. Norma's grandson, seven-year-old Gary, had just been placed in foster care. When I met with Norma, she related that she had been employed as a bookkeeper but has been out of work for four months. She was now living off unemployment benefits. Norma had looked for work, but no one was willing to pay anything close to what she had been earning. She had already dipped into savings (savings presumably earmarked for retirement) to make ends meet.

I met with Norma because I had hoped to move her grandson out of foster care and place her grandson with her. The law, as well as common sense, favors placement with family. I also had a vested interest in moving Gary out of foster care. The county had a shortage of foster homes, and placing Gary out of foster care would have freed up a spot in a foster home for another child.

However, even though she loved her grandson dearly, Norma was unwilling, even with foster care payments, to take Gary into her home. With the cost of after-school child care and other expenses, caring for her grandson would be an added expense. As her financial future was so uncertain, Norma felt she could not take on the moral and financial responsibility for her grandson. Her grandson remained in foster care.

In the decades since I met with Norma, the shortage of foster homes has only worsened. While regulations don't require foster parents to be homeowners, most foster parents are homeowners. As the cost of homeownership has escalated, the supply of foster homes has dwindled. The shortage of foster homes has become a crisis. Also, as more and more women are interested in careers, fewer women want to become foster mothers. (Only a handful of career-minded women become foster mothers, and while there are exceptions, foster fathers usually play a secondary role as foster parents).

Whether to care for a grandchild, an aging parent, or for some reason, family obligations keep millions of Americans, mostly women, from working. If they do work, they often work part-time, and part-time work usually pays less and does not come with benefits. Consequently, they have little to save for retirement. What can the government do to help?

A partial answer lies in state-managed IRA-like programs. California and some other states offer such plans. Under California's plan, if a company has five or more employees but does not have an IRA or other retirement plan, the employer registers its employees with the state-managed plan. For each employee, the first five percent of every paycheck is deducted and placed in the employee's retirement account. The first $1,000 saved is invested in a money market fund. After the employee has banked $1,000, the employee can direct savings into several different funds, including funds with specific ethical or environmental standards.

Participation is portable; if the employee changes job, the new employer simply informs the state. Like with the 401 (k) plan under a state-managed plan, the employer has no requirement to match the employee's contribution. Under such a plan, a person earning $35,000 a year, working for thirty years before any gain (or loss) from investments, would have $52,500. For someone who has lived close to the poverty level most of their life, fifty-two thousand dollars is a respectable amount of money.

Assuming an average of fifteen years of retirement, a retiree under a state-managed plan, would (before any loss or gain in investments) have about $3,500 a year to spend. Thirty-five hundred dollars is not a particularly large sum but does provide a little cushion against unexpected expenses.

As with IRAs and 401 (k) plans, some retirees under a state-managed will die before they have exhausted their retirement savings. The surviving spouse, which again is much more likely to be a woman than a man, will benefit from her husband's savings. If she then dies before the savings are exhausted, her children will benefit. The amount that her children will inherit will likely be significantly less than the affluent person who invested in an IRA or a 401 (k), but at least her children would get something. Therefore, a state-managed pension program, in a very modest way, provides for inherited wealth, wealth that reduces dependency on government.

To encourage states to establish state-managed pension funds, as it does for welfare, the federal government could pick up a large percentage of the cost. The cost of administering such plans is minimal. California's plan costs under $700,000 to operate annually, or less than the cost of a home in Los Angeles, San Francisco, or San Luis Obispo.

While not required, what if a three percent match was required for both 401 (k) plans and state-managed plans? No doubt, companies that currently don't provide a match would decry the expense. They would claim that they would just have to raise prices and that higher prices would reduce sales. This would be true --- to a point. The cost of labor usually a company's greatest expense but is rarely more than sixty percent of total operating costs. So, if a company normally sells a product for a hundred dollars, with sixty percent of the cost of the product cost being labor, a three percent match would mean a hundred dollar product would cost one hundred and one dollars – hardly an increase that would significantly affect sales.

As with so many other things, the number of years one has in retirement is related to race, gender, and education. The average life expectancy for whites is 79.1 years, but for African-Americans, it is 75.5 years. For all races combined, the average life expectancy for women is just over 81 years. For men, it is just over 76 years. Life expectancy is not reported based on educational attainment, but overall mortality is. The mortality rate of college-educated women is 146 deaths per 100,000. For college-educated men, it is 214. For women with a high school diploma, the rate is 322 deaths per 100,000, and for men with no more than a high school diploma, it is a whopping 596 deaths per 100,000.

Part of the huge discrepancy in life expectancy is due to lifestyle choices, in particular, smoking. The college-educated are less likely to smoke than the less educated. Moreover, those working at a modest-paying job (twice the poverty rate) are half as likely to smoke as those living at the poverty level (16% v 32%). Smoking does generate tax revenue, but taxes on cigarettes vary widely. In the District of Columbia, the tax is $4.50 per pack. In Georgia, the tax is thirty-seven cents per pack. The average state tax is $1.73. Collectively, the states earn roughly twenty billion dollars a year from taxes on tobacco. The federal government last raised taxes on cigarettes in 2009. The current federal excise tax on a pack of cigarettes is now a dollar a pack. The federal government earns about twelve billion dollars a year from taxes on tobacco.

Decades ago, the average age for a diagnosis of lung cancer was sixty-six. The average is now seventy-one. Presumably, with higher taxes, those who smoked now smoked less, and it took a longer time for lung cancer to develop. Since the average age of diagnosis is seventy-one, the vast majority of those on Medicaid who have lung cancer are retired. Treating elderly poor cancer patients is expensive (and recall that, unlike Medicare, patients on Medicaid pay nothing for their medical care). The cost to treat a single patient for lung cancer can easily run into the tens of thousands of dollars. A cost only partially offset by the taxes the patient has paid on cigarettes.

Imposing even higher taxes on cigarettes would fall disproportionately on the poor but would also increase their lifespan. Imposing higher taxes to discourage smoking is the moral thing to do. It also makes economic sense. In comparison to a smoker, the non-smoker rarely dies of lung cancer, heart disease, and other smoking-related diseases that are expensive to treat.

As the elderly have greater medical needs, their medical costs are greater. As they live longer, women use more health dollars than men. Over their respective lifetimes, the average cost of medical care for a woman is about a third more than that of a man. About forty percent of this additional lifetime cost is due to women living longer; the rest, *sixty percent,* is due to the simple fact, even excluding maternity costs, women have more health needs than men. However, unlike auto insurance and life insurance, where men pay more because they are in more accidents and live shorter lives, it is illegal to base medical insurance premiums on gender. So, in the 21St century, men are chivalrously picking up a good portion of the tab for women's health care.

The quality of life, especially for the elderly, is one of the most important factors in medical decision-making. Cost is certainly another factor. Let's consider a hypothetical case of an eighty-three-year-old woman whom we will call Nell. Nell's husband died five years ago. Nell lives comfortably, if modestly, on her $1,500 monthly Social Security check. She has $30,000 in a savings account. (Thirty thousand dollars is the *average* savings account balance, the *average* being more than four times the median).

The closest of Nell's children live three hours away, and the rest live even further away. As Nell no longer drives, the only time when she sees her children or grandchildren is when they come to visit her. As she no longer drives, Nell gets rides from friends to church and wherever else she needs to go. Further, in the past few years, Nell has been using her walker more and more. Also, Nell used to watch *Jeopardy* every night but no longer does so; it just became too frustrating to watch. She could not answer the questions fast enough, even ones she was pretty sure she knew.

Nell's doctor tells her she has a serious medical condition and needs treatment. To treat her condition, Nell will have to spend a few days in the hospital, endure a fair amount of discomfort, and go to several follow-up appointments. The procedure her doctor proposes has a fifty-fifty chance of adding five years to her life, but if not successful, Nell will likely die within six months. The doctor can't estimate the cost, but Nell knows that even with Medicare, the medical procedure will cost her a good portion of her life savings. Whenever she dies, Nell wants her savings evenly distributed among her five grandchildren.

What does Nell do? Does she gamble her grandchildren's inheritance for a fifty-fifty chance of living longer? What would she do if there was only a five percent chance of success? Some "Nells," especially if the chances for a successful outcome were slim, would consider the expense, discomfort, and stress of the medical procedure just too much. They would decline treatment and save their life savings for the grandchildren. Would Nell's answer be different if she was poor, on Medicaid, and her medical care was completely free? Your author would like an APA-style research study to find out.

Let's say, for the sake of argument, an APA-style study showed those whose health care is completely free are more apt to choose (expensive) aggressive medical intervention than those who spend their own money (or their grandchildren's inheritance). How would the government use such information?

To answer that question, we first need to consider private health plans. Under private health plans, patients get notices from their insurance companies that read something like, "your recent stay at Mercy Hospital cost $46,347. Your share of cost is $3,281. Payment is expected upon demand." The poor should be treated no differently. They need to know that their "free treatment" isn't really free. Just as Nell considered her grandchildren's inheritance in making a medical decision, the poor should be informed of the cost of their "free" medical care.

Of course, it is cheaper to prevent disease than to cure disease. How, then, could the poor, particularly the elderly poor, be motivated to seek preventative care? Money is the obvious answer; give the elderly poor cash bonuses for getting flu shots. Despite free flu shots being commonplace, in a typical year, about 145,000 older Americans are hospitalized for the flu.

Paying the poor to get vaccinated is a win-win. The poor would get a little extra cash, and the cost of flu-related hospitalization is decreased. The same reward system could be used be for cancer and other health screenings. When treated early, the survival rate for cancer is higher, and the costs lower. Further, men are far more reluctant to obtain medical care than women. However, if given the financial motivation to do so, more men will seek preventive care, and their life expectancy will begin to catch up with that of women.

Of course, eventually, everyone dies. However, there is something especially tragic about a senior citizen dying by their own hand. Men aged sixty-five and older commit suicide at six times the rate of women (31 to 5 per 100,000 population). To reduce the high suicide rate of men in their retirement years, the government *could* hire a legion of mental health professionals specially dedicated to helping the needs of elderly men. However, finding enough mental health professionals that understand the needs of older men might be difficult. Since 2013, twice as many women have become psychologists than men. Moreover, psychological treatment is expensive, an hourly rate of $150/hour is not unusual, and a psychologist can see only so many clients in a week.

A common-sense finding in mental health research is that individuals who have social activities are less likely to feel depressed and have suicidal thoughts. Communities with recreational programs specifically for senior men (e.g., senior men's golf, senior men's tennis, etc.) might have lower suicide rates than cities that don't have such programs. Again, this is another area where an APA-style study would be helpful.

However, presumably, recreational programs for senior men would go only so far in reducing their suicide rate. Olden men, men who worked most of their adult lives, need the dignity of meaningful, *paid* employment. Of course, volunteer opportunities abound for seniors. Churches and charities "love" the "free labor" that retirees can provide. However, that the labor is free is the point. If you sell a well-used car for $5,000, it still has some value. Offer to give away a well-used car away for free the car is obviously worthless. No one wants to feel worthless.

Like churches and other charities, schools greatly appreciate the free labor that volunteers can provide. However, volunteers in schools are overwhelming are women. Yet, a male volunteer can be such a benefit for a boy. One boy in my caseload, who was in the seventh grade, was nearly illiterate. Yet, after meeting regularly with an older male tutor for a few months, the boy could read at near grade level.

Sadly, the boy had to be moved to another foster home, and his tutor/mentor could no longer meet with him. For the last few years of his high school education, your author was the closest thing to a father figure this young man had. However, unlike the mentor who was there two to three times a week, because of the demands of other cases, your author could only meet with the young man once or twice a month. It was not enough. In his senior year in high school, the young man started making bad decisions. He was repeatedly arrested, and as a young adult, even briefly went to prison. An outcome that likely would have been prevented if his mentor/tutor had been able to continue with him.

To get more men to tutor/mentor boys in school is simple. Pay them. Just as it does for school lunches, the federal government could reimburse local school districts specifically to hire older men as tutors. Government programs are generally not allowed to discriminate on sex or race. However, set-aside programs are constitutional if they are targeted to address some inequity. Older men committing suicide at six times the rate of older women and boys dropping out of schools much more than girls are social inequities that need addressing.

Providing financial incentives for older men to work part-time tutoring/mentoring in schools would be a bargain. A hundred million hours of tutoring at fifteen dollars an hour equates to a relatively modest 1.5 billion dollars. For the relatively low cost of 1.5 billion dollars, the government buys not one but two bridges. One "bridge" that reduces the high dropout rate for boys and another that reduces the high suicide rate in older men.

Of course, most seniors do not contemplate suicide in their golden years. In retirement, the affluent take cruises and otherwise enjoy "the good life." Moreover, unlike the elderly poor, even the moderately wealthy do not have to worry about having gas money to visit the grandchildren.

In retirement, if both spouses had high-paying jobs, they can receive over $6,000 in social security benefits a month. With high-paying jobs, they likely contributed to IRA or 401 k plans. The average

IRA balance for those approaching retirement (i.e., ages 55 to 64) is $104,000. The average balance in a 401 (k) is a whopping $496,000. (The median is $292,000). Some retirees, obviously, are quite wealthy. When they die, their children will inherit considerable wealth.

A common maxim from financial advisors is "don't outlive your money." However, for those who, in their working years had modest-paying, but "honest jobs," saving for retirement was a luxury. They can easily outlive the money they put away in their savings account at an FDIC-insured bank. As previously noted, nine percent of retirees in America poor enough to receive food stamps. Retirement in America should not mean food stamps, or even worse, worrying if the local "meals on wheels" program will arrive on time. A state-managed pension program is a small price to provide some dignity to the retiree who toiled a minimum-wage job or, due to a family obligation, passed on taking a better-paying job.

With a few modest and inexpensive changes, such as not taxing unemployment benefits and not taxing state refunds, providing financial incentives for preventative care, and mandating state-managed pensions, mandating a minimum three-percent match from employers, the lives of the elderly poor could be improved in a substantive fashion. These changes, in a small way, would offset the loss of private-sector pensions. The base of the pyramid would narrow just a little.

CHAPTER NINE

THE AMERICAN DREAM IN THE 21ST CENTURY

Homeownership provides a sense of belonging. Having a home of one's own provides a sense of permanence that a rented home or apartment does not. Having a sense of permanence, of having a place of your own, is a large part of the American Dream.

Homeownership makes for safe neighborhoods. In areas where the rate of homeownership is high, the crime rate is low. When the "neighborhood" is a large public housing project, where no one even has the opportunity to buy, the crime rate is high.

Homeownership provides inherited wealth and prevents poverty in the next generation.

Homeownership, like much of America, has a racial divide. Seventy-two percent of white households own their home. For Hispanic households, the homeownership rate is about 48% and about 42% for African-American households -- percentages that have changed little since 1994.

In 1965, the median household income was just over $7,000, and few women had high-earning professional jobs. In 1965, the household income was primarily, if not exclusively, the man's income. In 1965, the median price of a home was just over $20,000, or about three times the median income. In 2019, the median household income was $63,000. Now, more often than not, for home buyers, the median household income is based on two wage-earners. In 2019, the median price of a home was $325,000, or more than four times the household income.

So, in 2019, it took two incomes to earn a fourth of the cost of a home, when in 1965, it took one income to earn a third.

Homeownership is related to educational level. In higher-priced cities, it often takes the income from a job that requires a college degree to afford a home. As, for the past two decades, women have outnumbered men in college, it is not surprising then, according to Lending Tree, single women now own 1.5 million more homes than single men.

Those who can't afford to buy a home rent. In 1970, the median for a year's worth of rent was just under eighteen percent of income. In 2017, the median for a years' worth of rent was twenty percent of household income. A two percent increase might not seem like much, but the gap grows wider each year. Moreover, statistics alone do not tell the whole story. A young family that can't find affordable housing might move in with their parents. If the adults combine their incomes to pay rent, economically speaking, this is a household where rent is considered "affordable" -- not a young family priced out of the rental market.

As a social worker, your author has mostly worked with men and women at the lower end of the income/educational spectrum. Men and women with little education beyond high school (and sometimes not even that). Men and women who did not have vocational skills. Men and women who worked at minimum wage jobs or worked under the table or worked at no legitimate job at all. Men and women that often turned to illicit drugs to escape their desperate circumstances. Men (and a few women) who took their frustrations out on their children or, more commonly, their significant other. These men and women needed drug counseling and anger management but also needed the sense of self-worth that comes from having a respectable job.

Two buzzwords in the social services system are "outreach" and "partnership." "Outreach" is conducted to ensure that those legally entitled to benefits apply for benefits. "Partnership" is needed to help ensure coordination with other government agencies and nongovernmental agencies providing services to the poor. However, social service agencies do very little "outreach" or "partnering" with the profit-making world. Even something as simple as posting job notices on a bulletin board can run amok of bureaucratic rules.

Typically, a bulletin board in the lobby of a welfare office is adorned with flyers about parenting classes, where to get mental health treatment, the legal rights of applicants, and so on. Only very occasionally are there postings about job openings. Moreover, in California, if by chance there is a job posting, the job posting must be posted in English and Spanish --- even if the job requires fluency in English. Such a rule discourages employers who need English-speaking employees to be good corporate citizens and use the welfare office for recruiting efforts.

As noted in chapter two, the federal government, in the form of tax incentives, "reaches out" to the private sector by providing tax incentives to businesses that serve impoverished communities. Taxes, however, are a relatively modest amount of a company's total overhead. Usually, a company's greatest cost is the cost of labor. (Automobile companies pay significantly more for their employees' health insurance than they do for steel). As taxes make up only a moderate portion of a company's expenses, tax incentives can only help so far in getting the poor employed.

What is needed is more "outreach" and "partnership" from the welfare department to the private sector. For example, directors of local welfare departments should be required to meet periodically with managers/owners of local employers to develop action plans. These action plans could include job fairs, establishing commuter van service, mentor programs, etc.

As noted in previous chapters, other changes in government policy are needed as well. Welfare-to-work rules need to be modified so that parents have sufficient time to complete a training or certification program that will lead to genuine economic self-sufficiency. Food stamp allocations need to be age-based. School districts need financial incentives to offer free breakfast to needy students. Title IX regulations need to be invoked so that local school districts address the gender discrepancy in the dropout rate. Financial incentives are needed to increase the supply of daycare providers. State-managed pension plans need to be available in every state. Government-financed "sweat equity" housing programs are needed to supplement the FHA program.

So the unemployed don't become the unhoused capitalism in the 21St century also needs to change. Corporations need financial incentives to hire the unemployed. Tax incentives are also needed to encourage large companies to offer employee-owned housing. Tax code changes are needed for the construction of more owner-occupied housing. A modest sales tax on the sale of stock is needed to promote investment over pure profit-making. A modest sales tax on luxury goods is also warranted. But most of all, modifying 21st Century capitalism means upholding the US-backed United Nations Declaration of Human Rights that workers are entitled to "just compensation." "Just compensation" should equate to an ordinary "hard-working" American family being able to afford a home, however modest, of their own.

While changes are needed in both the public and private sectors, there also needs to be a change in the American mindset. The 19th Century belief system that anyone in American with a good work ethic can go from "rags to riches" is no longer viable. Even for the very talented and hard-working, there are fewer and fewer opportunities. A high school GPA of 4.0 is no longer a guarantee of admission to a top-tier college like Harvard, Yale, Stanford, or UCLA. Even a state university like Cal Poly San Luis Obispo denies admission to over *ten thousand* high school graduates with 4.0 GPAs or better. Students who, in past generations, would have been accepted at a top-tier college now settle for a lower-tier college. They bump out the merely well-qualified and so on down the educational system.

In the working world, those with top-tier jobs can afford to live in "McMansions" in gated communities. Others, not quite so fortunate, have to suffice with a nice house in a good neighborhood with good schools. With the ever-increasing demand high for "good housing," prices continue to climb. With the median home now costing over $325,000, even those with good-paying "honest jobs" are bumped out of homeownership. Millions of hard-working Americans can't even afford to purchase a home on the "wrong side" of railroad tracks.

Other 19th century needs to be abandoned as well. In 1875, the Statue of Liberty was erected and said to the world, "Give us your tired, your poor, your huddled masses yearning to breathe free." It was immigrant labor (mostly Chinese and Irish) that built the railroads. In the early part of the 20th century, it was mostly immigrants and the sons of immigrants that built skyscrapers and manned assembly lines. When the Statue of Liberty was erected in 1875, there were fewer than fifty million people were living in the entire United States -- *millions less* than the number of poor people in the United States today. Moreover, with technological advances and global market forces, there are proportionally fewer good-paying jobs to be had. Simply put, in the 21st Century, America doesn't need the level of immigration it needed in the 19th and early 20th century.

For some, as most immigrants are non-white, calling for immigration control is racism by another name. However, the law of supply and demand knows no race. If the "supply" of legal and illegal cheap labor is high, wage growth is minimal. If the supply of labor is low, wages go up. A liberal immigration policy depresses wages for unskilled labor jobs (jobs disproportionally held by non-whites), while a restrictive immigration policy pushes wages up.

Moreover, as the supply of housing is finite, a liberal immigration policy pushes up the cost of rent. A restrictive immigration policy helps keep rents from escalating. As renters are disproportionately non-white, a liberal immigration policy is disproportionately harmful to minorities. Two steps in immigration reform would be to require that welfare payments for children be paid to a US citizen and bring back (and properly administer) the Bracero program.

In 1965, when the War on Poverty started, the United States produced thirty-eight percent of the world's output. In 2020, it was less than fifteen percent. In 2024, it is expected that China's GDP will surpass that of the US. As America's share of the world economy continues to shrink, China will assert more and more financial and political muscle.

In 1965, China's life expectancy was just under fifty years; now, it is nearly seventy. China's population is expected to peak in 2029 and then begin to shrink. Japan and several European countries already have a negative birth/death rate. However, for the foreseeable future, America's population, *for the poorest one-third*, is expected to continue to grow. From population growth alone the base will get wider and the apex narrower. The demand for housing, particularly housing for the less affluent will continue to increase. However, as demand increases so does price. As price increase the percentage of Americans that can afford to own their home will decrease. Fewer heirs will inherit equity. The base of the pyramid will get wider and the apex narrower.

Even before the pandemic, America already owed China well over one *trillion* dollars. At a three percent interest rate, the annual cost of such debt is sixty billion dollars. Not including the cost of government overhead, sixty billion dollars would, at ten thousand dollars a year, pay for six million Section 8 vouchers.

Even before the stimulus spending because of the pandemic, from all sources, China, European banks, US banks, foreign and domestic investors, the US debt was already twenty-two *trillion* dollars. The interest payment *alone* on that debt is four hundred billion dollars a year or the entire budget for the food stamps, school lunch, and school breakfast programs for over five years.

In the late 19th century, there were 80,000 "paupers" living in almshouses and poorhouses. In 2019, even with the anti-poverty program of the 1960s, 360,000 Americans, mostly women and children, lived in homeless shelters. Adjusted for population growth, the percentage of American's living in homeless shelters in the 21st century is roughly *double* the number that lived in almshouses in the 19th century. Moreover, that 360,000 figure does not count the 195,000, mostly men, who can't even call a homeless shelter a home. Their "home" is under an overpass, a creek bed, or some random stretch of sidewalk.

Tens of billions of dollars are needed to properly house the poor. Those tens of billions can come from two sources increasing taxes or taking on more debt. As we have seen, there is a limit to raising taxes. However, if properly spent, taking on more debt can yield a good ROI (return on investment). So that the cycle of poverty is broken, more money for housing (and other services) for the poor is needed.

While tens of billions are needed to provide housing and other social services are needed for the poor, it is also critical to realize there is just so much livable land. In 1970, the population of Los Angeles was 2.8 million; in 2010, it was 3.7 million --- a million more people living in the same amount of space. In 1970, the population of California was 19.9 million. In 2018 it was 39.4 million. The population doubled, but the size of California remained the same. More people in the same about of space means a greater demand for housing. As rents are so high in California, nearly twenty percent of Californians live in functional poverty.

The housing crisis is not just in California. From 1970 to 2020, the population of Austin, Texas, increased from 267,000 to 806,000, a more than three-fold increase. During the same period, Texas' population doubled from a little over eleven million to over twenty-five million. From 1970 to 2010, Delaware's population grew from 550,000 to 890,000. Alaska's population more than doubled from 302,000 to over 902,000, and forty percent of Alaska's population lives in just one city, Anchorage. In 1970, the median cost of a home in Anchorage was less than $60,000. In 2019, it was $240,000.

Rich or poor, housing is usually a family's greatest expense. However, if a poor person is sick and needs (government-funded) hospitalization, just a few days in the hospital can cost the equivalent of a few years' worth of taxpayer's dollars for housing subsidies, cash aid, food stamps, etc. Rewarding the poor with a few million dollars for preventative care could save billions.

But whether paying for housing, medical care, food programs, or subsidized daycare, incurring debt to pay for such services for the poor is subject to mathematical reality. Borrowing five hundred billion, *each year*, for the needs of seventy-five million poor people, not counting government overhead, equates to twenty thousand dollars of assistance (medical care, cash aid etc.) for a family of three (e.g. mother and two children). If that seventy-five million reaches one hundred million, for a family of three, before government overheard, benefits are just $15,000 -- an amount way below the poverty level. However, if the number of poor is fifty million, then for a family of three, that five hundred billion, before government overhead, equates to $30,000 worth of assistance.

Most Americans, however, do not see helping the poor in mathematical terms or as a function of America's indebtedness to China and other countries or competition between "guns versus butter" or food stamps versus National Parks. They see helping the poor as a moral obligation. For the faithful, helping the poor is both a duty and an expression of their faith. However, volunteering (or working) at a homeless shelter or food bank, while noble, does not create wealth. Capitalism creates wealth. However, greedy capitalism creates resentment and anger. An individual who earns 1/500 of the CEO or who has no job at all might be tempted to employ extra-legal, even violent, means to even things out.

The 1960s, which brought the War on Poverty, also brought the Apollo moon project. Going to the moon was only possible with lots of money, good planning, and a myriad of decisions, large and small. In the race to the moon, a small "wrong decision" can and did prove to have deadly consequences.

However, with social programs, small bad decisions usually don't spell disaster. A small decision, good or bad, has little effect on the overall poverty rate or the rate of homeownership. Still, even small decisions can make a difference. A school district that invokes Title IX regulations for gender equality in graduation rates, requires less fiction and more nonfiction in English classes, requires a semester of ethics for graduation and provides free breakfast, and more free lunches to its needy students will graduate more and better students, students who are better prepared for the labor market of the 21st century.

In school districts where gender equality as required under Title IX is not addressed, where English is taught as it always has been, where there is no free breakfast, and free lunch is an after-thought, fewer students will graduate. These non-graduates will be disproportionately non-white males. Such young men (and women), if they find work, will work at lower-paying jobs. Being unemployed or working at lower-paying jobs, they will pay little in taxes, but in the form of food stamps, medical care, etc. They will, however, consume many tax dollars.

For those working at lower-paying jobs, given the high cost of rent -- even for a modest apartment or mobile home in a rundown trailer park– a month's worth of earnings can exceed a months' rent. To make ends meet, some, either as a supplement to their legitimate job or as their primary source of "income," will turn to crime. Most eventually will get arrested and convicted. Their criminal records will make it all the more difficult for them to find decent-paying jobs and become taxpayers instead of tax users. Given the high cost, both direct and indirect, of crime, *even if it means more debt,* the economic benefit of modifying government policies, tax codes, etc., is a good return on investment. It is also the right moral choice.

The proposed changes in the preceding chapters are largely independent of each other, i.e., a change in the tax code is not related to how food stamps are allocated or how English is taught in high school. But that is how progress is made, breaking a big problem into manageable action items. Not every idea proposed will find universal support, and few readers will accept every idea. For those readers in a position of power, support those changes in which you do believe. Any change for the better helps. To broaden support for the various ideas, whenever possible, both moral and economic rationales have been given.

If the political will is only found to adopt the free and less expensive ideas, the poor will have a better bridge, but not the most cost-effective one taxpayers deserve. But whether in the collection and distribution of child support, modifying the tax code, or how food support programs are administered, each policy change means better mileage from taxpayers' dollars. More importantly, it also means some will be lifted out of poverty. Some might even be able to afford a home of their own, or, at least, their children will have a better chance at the American Dream of homeownership.

Still, whether built for the open market or the poor, with each new housing tract or apartment complex, the quantity of available land to build housing grows smaller. As supply dwindles, demand grows, and prices go up. As the population increases, a home, whether purchased or rented at an affordable price, becomes more and more elusive for more and more Americans.

If America continues with its current policies and the population continues to grow, the number of Americans calling a homeless shelter or a bridge underpass "home" will continue to grow. If little or nothing is done, by the end of the 21st century, hundreds of thousands, if not millions, of Americans will be worse off than the paupers of the 19th century who, at least, could call the poorhouse home.

NOTES

Preface:

In my thirty-four year career in social services, the number of single-parent households on welfare in my caseload headed by a father was in the single digits. If a man was in the home with the mother, he was likely a live-in boyfriend, not a husband. He might or not have been the father of any of the children.

Chapter 1: A brief history of capitalism and public assistance

In other parts of the country, when a car has stopped a light, a man will offer to clean a motorist's windshield for change. In southern California, sometimes, instead of oranges, vendors sell flowers.

In larger states, TANF is administered at the county level with state supervision.

The bidding process is, of course, far more complicated. For example, environmental impact and feasibility studies are needed. However, for the purposes here, such details are not relevant.

As AFDC became TANF, food stamps became SNAP (Supplemental Nutrition Assistance Program). However, in everyday use, SNAP has not caught on as a term.

Chapter 2: Work ethic, moral compass, dads, and education

I had a couple of cases where the parents were married and neither used illicit substances. In these cases, the mothers had "Horatio Alger Jobs," but the fathers couldn't find steady legitimate work. Without their wife's knowledge, these fathers, because they wanted to contribute to the household income, took to drug dealing.

Prenatal exposure to alcohol or illicit substance can also affect brain development and impact a child's ability to develop a moral compass. There are, of course, other factors which affect brain development.

As church attendance has declined, so has the use of pastoral counseling. Now instead of turning to clergy for help, more and more individuals see a licensed therapist. The increased demand for mental health services increases the cost of both private and public insurance. Many clergy, as part of their compensation, are provided free housing. Such housing is tax-free. Some say this favors religion over atheism. However, from a purely business point of view, it makes sense for the government to "incentivize" pastoral counseling by allowing clergy to receive their housing tax-free. An individual or couple who has benefited from pastoral counseling may feel compelled to "pay it forward." An individual or couple that has, in the form of co-payments, deductibles, and insurance premiums, paid for their mental health treatment is not as inclined to "pay it forward," and larger society suffers. (Of course, unlicensed pastoral counseling is not a substitute for licensed care of mental health disorders. However, for ordinary problems, pastoral counseling has benefitted many).

There are also economies of scale for the government in a two-parent household. If there are two poor households, a food stamp worker opens two cases, and another government employee opens a child support case. In a low-income two-parent household, there is just a single food stamp case.

I told Tricia her vacuum cleaner probably just needed a new belt and that I was sure she could do it herself. She did fix the vacuum cleaner on her own.

Some might say the absent parent should be required to attend parenting classes, but that would be counter-productive. When one is forced to do something, a common reaction is resentment. Someone harboring resentment about having "to be in this stupid class" will likely learn little. If given a financial incentive non-custodial fathers (and non-custodial mothers) will be far more receptive to learning than if attendance is compulsory.

In his autobiography, *Cry Like a Man*, Jason Wilson vividly writes about the pain of growing up in a poor African-American neighborhood without a father. As an adult, Jason Wilson found faith and "Horatio Alger" jobs. He got married and, unlike his wife, never completed college. With an ever-increasing belief in God, Wilson established what would become a nationally recognized youth program.

As part of their recovery, many parents found faith; specifically, one of the tenets in Alcoholic Anonymous is a belief in a higher power.

I don't recall why, but for some reason, an after-school program was not available for Cameron. Also, Cameron did not have grandfathers or uncles who could substitute as a father figure.

There is a school edition of *Born a Crime*.

Chapter 3: Food programs and Homeland Security

To receive food stamps the bum has to apply. That puts him in touch with "the system." A caseworker might be able to nudge the bum into treatment. Outside "the system," the bum has less of a chance of entering treatment.

Technically, a child born to foreign nationals in the United States has dual citizenship, US citizenship, and the citizenship of the parents.

Cash aid and food stamps currently go to the non-citizen for the benefit of the child. However, medical care is specific for the child. For instance, on Medicaid, the citizen-child can get eyeglasses for free, but the non-citizen sibling cannot. The same is true for prescription medication and dental care.

Emergency medical services are provided to the noncitizen. Hospitals are required by law to provide emergency service without respect to citizenship or insurance. (Just like Americans traveling abroad would be provided emergency care if needed). Prenatal care is also covered; the economic rationale being a woman who receives prenatal care is more likely to deliver a healthy (and less expensive) baby.

Historically, as noted in the first chapter, local government paid for the medical care for the indigent, which is why there are so many "county general" hospitals. However, medical care can be extremely expensive. For a small county, just a couple of patients receiving expensive medical can severely strain a local government's budget. Like counties elsewhere, because of the cost, San Luis Obispo County closed its "county general." Additionally, local governments are constitutionally required to provide medical care for inmates in county jails. Such care can be a considerable expense and difficult to provide. It is not only the cost of providing the care, but if an inmate needs medical care outside of the jail, there is the cost of supervising the inmate at the hospital or clinic receiving medical care (e.g. an x-ray) that cannot be provided in the jail. The cost to provide medical care for inmates in state and federal prisons is tens of billions of dollars.

Chapter 4: Public housing, crime, and homeownership

In San Luis Obispo County, there was no Habit for Humanity program, but a local self-help housing operated in a manner similar to Habit for Humanity. However, for child welfare cases, unlike public housing, there was no consideration for further reunification by providing housing. Intact and otherwise more worthy families were given assistance.

To help youth transition to independent adulthood, many states now allow for extended foster care after the youth legally becomes an adult. At age eighteen, most youths in foster care are ill-prepared to be self-supporting adults. With extended foster care, as young adults, former foster children, are less likely to be homeless, engage in criminal activity, and get pregnant (or father a child). The government, of course, has a moral duty to help former foster children lead successful lives as adults. Moral obligations aside, another argument for funding extended foster care, is that is cost-effective. Extended foster care decreases the chances that young adults will engage in criminal behavior to make ends meet or have children they cannot afford to raise without government support.

In Hawaii, at least two state parks have been taken over by transients, and so, are unsuitable for most tourists or locals to enjoy.

Chapter 5: Poverty, parenting, and child care

The term child welfare court cases is used to distinguish family court from juvenile (criminal) court. Juvenile court usually refers to youth who are charged with committing a crime. Family court generally refers to ordinary divorce and custody cases. (As unmarried parents are so common, the term "divorce court" is not used anymore). In California, child welfare cases are heard in dependency court, and the child can be legally referred to as dependent of the juvenile court.

However, in many states, the child, legally, is referred to as a CINS (child in need of services). In some states, child welfare cases are heard, in closed court, by a family court judge.

In all states, juveniles who commit crimes, except for petty offenses like underage smoking, are entitled to counsel.

Parents who successfully completed treatment and had their parental rights restored were usually slightly better off financially than before their children entered "the system." Still, virtually none were homeowners. Foster parents almost always are homeowners and, financially, are much better off than the birth parents.

The term "successfully" means genuine recovery. Some with substance abuse problems can complete a treatment program and relapse within a year, a month, or even a week.

In child welfare cases, adoption by an extended family member is quite common. Typically the relative who adopts has a high standard of living than the biological parents but a lower standard of living than the typical foster family.

Just to be clear, funding for children already in child care continued.

Before a foster home is licensed or a home approved as adoptive placement, child welfare runs criminal record checks. In a *very, very small* minority of cases, foster parents and adoptive parents do, later on, commit crimes.

The 233,000 number of child care providers includes child care providers of all types. Small family child care centers (e.g., daycare operated in a person's) home is about half the total number.

Chapter 6: The apex and base of the pyramid

Capitalist Hong Kong also taxes the sale of stock.

Chapter 7: The changing workforce, market forces, and welfare reform

Like most cartoons and television shows of the era, all the characters in *The Jetsons* were white. Cartoons and television shows of the 21st century are thankful more culturally diverse.

General cargo does not include commodities like oil, natural gas, or iron, etc.

Not all longshoremen work as crane operators.

Almost all communities now have garbage sorted into trash and recycle, and sometimes green waste. Having two or three cans to collect means waste collection takes longer, resulting in a greater demand for garbage collectors.

Teachers in charter schools do not enjoy the same civil service protection.

Technically, court stenographers, at least in California, are not government employees. They are paid as contractors. However, they enjoy considerable job security and can earn bonuses by providing printed transcripts they prepare outside of court hours.

The post office's workforce is forty-five percent female.

The International Ladies Garment Workers union merged with the AFL-CIO in 1995.

Some academic research corroborates common thinking that more attractive waitresses are tipped more, especially by men. By extension, it is logical to extrapolate that male waiters are tipped less by men and, unless particularly handsome, are tipped less by women.

One of the "factors" for manufacturing decline is that automobiles last much longer than in past generations. With cars lasting longer, there is less demand for new automobiles.

There are robots that deliver medicines from one part of the hospital to the other and perform other simple tasks.

Unlike other professional schools that are now majority female, dental schools are nearly evenly split by gender.

The 700,000 total includes limousine drivers.

While the technology for driverless cars is not too far off, it is doubtful that driverless vehicles that carry passengers will be commonplace anytime soon. Buses, trains, and presumably driverless cars are "public conveyances" and, as such, have a very high legal obligation to operate safely.

The solar and wind industries now employ more people than coal. However, for both solar and wind farms, most of the labor is needed in initial construction, often away from urban centers. The coal mine provided steady work for a nearby town. The man or woman working on constructing a solar or wind farm has a short-term job assignment with a long commute, while historically, the coal miner had a steady job close to home

The FAA defines a commercial pilot as anyone earning money from flying. This includes private pilot instructors. Pilots flying scheduled air routes are certified with the far more stringent standard of Airline Transport Pilot.

Commercial fishing is another almost universally male job. However, fishermen are often paid by shares; a deckhand gets one share, the Captain has multiple shares. There is just about as much work involved in bringing in a big catch as a small one. Fishing seasons are heavily regulated. Both because the size of the catch can vary considerably and employment is seasonal, income security from working as a (male or female) fisherman is minimal.

Morticians and funeral directors are male-dominated vocations, and as everybody eventually dies, their is job security. However, as more and more are opting for cremation instead of a traditional burial, employment in the funeral industry is not as lucrative as in the past.

One private-sector occupation that requires no college degree, relatively little specialized training, and is nearly split gender-wise (53% female, 47% male) and is highly dependent on the economy is that of a real estate agent. However, as costs of housing skyrocketed, commissions per house sold have increased.

For simplicity, I refer only to trial court appointments, not elevation to an appellate court.

Medical care is not completely independent of market forces. In Border States, many Americans obtain routine medical care or fill their prescriptions in Mexico. Others because of cost, opt to have surgery in Mexico and other countries.

There were other issues other than extreme poverty that led to the children's removal, but if Rosalie had received welfare for a family of five, the impact of these other issues would have been less. (For reasons of confidentiality, I cannot be more specific).

Rosalie's children thrived in foster care. Still, I did no doubt that Rosalie loved her children and, given her circumstances, did her best.

I had another case where the parents were developmentally delayed. They did their best too, but again their best still lead to neglect.

Automobile mechanics are not as dependent on the economy as aircraft mechanics. In a poor economy, fewer new cars are sold, so more maintenance for older cars is needed.

At least according to my female co-workers, Jim was not exceptionally handsome. Why would a woman be interested in an unemployed and not a particularly handsome man? Given the mothers' drug problems, it is likely that Jim was a drug dealer, and his girlfriends traded sex for drugs.

It should be remembered that whites, whether rich, middle-class, or poor, are the largest ethnic group. As the largest ethnic group their population growth contributes the most to the widening of the base of the wealth pyramid.

Calculating the total cost for the children in foster care is difficult. There is the direct cost of foster care payments, as well as the salaries of social workers and their supervisors, general overhead expenses, court costs, and so on.

The figure of $200,000 is an estimate. There are the direct costs of welfare payments, medical care, etc., but also overhead expenses.

Recipients could opt-out of receiving free condoms.

The prefrontal cortex forms slightly earlier in women.

Full-time college students, who are childless, would not be eligible any tax credit under a modified Earned Income Credit program.

Chapter 8: The three-legged stool meets the 21St century

Before automated milking machines, a three-legged stool was common on dairy farms. With automated milking machines, fewer farmers are needed to milk cows. However, if hand labor were still needed to milk cows, the price of milk would be exorbitant.

Having two classes of retirement benefits also occurs in the public sector. Public employees hired after a certain date contribute less to their pensions and receiving correspondingly lower benefits.

ERISA also required employers to follow specific accounting regulations regarding their pension plans. Also, much like how the FDIC insures banks, ERISA created the Pension Benefit Guaranty Board (PBGB) to insure pension funds.

For 2020, as part of the stimulus package because of the pandemic, the first $10,000 in unemployment benefits was untaxed. This one-time benefit should be permanent.

Foster care benefits usually do not cover the full cost of caring for a child.

I suspect the popularity and low price of financial software rendered the grandmother's job obsolete.

I do not mean to imply that the shortage of foster homes should be blamed on women who seek careers. That more women are opting for careers instead of being stay-at-home moms with their children or caring for children in daycare or foster care is simply a demographic reality. Also, as any working parent knows, juggling work while raising a family is difficult. With foster children, for a variety of reasons juggling work and parenting is even more challenging.

The employee can opt out of the plan or have a different amount deducted.

In the early part of the 21st century, many states raised taxes on cigarettes.

Technically, the federal tax on tobacco is by weight, not by the pack. The amount of tax is very nearly equal to a dollar a pack.

The figure of $137,000 was the amount in 2020. The figure is periodically adjusted upward, but the concept that the particularly affluent pay no additional tax remains unchanged.

During the pandemic, some states, with limited success, offered financial incentives to be vaccinated.

Only a few states allow physician-assisted suicide, so the number of men (and women) committing suicide due to a terminal illness is very low.

Chapter 9: The American Dream and social services

So that a welfare recipient might find a job more easily, many nonprofits provide interview clothes or haircuts to welfare recipients. In San Luis Obispo County, the welfare department provides vouchers to hair salons and low-cost retail clothing stores. There is strict control over the vouchers. The taxpayers' money is spent wisely. It is a system other welfare agencies should adopt.

Your author worked as a recruiter for the census bureau and learned first-hand about the "must post in Spanish" rule. While the census needed enumerators who spoke English and Spanish, posting in Spanish falsely implied that only fluency in Spanish was required.

A GPA of greater than 4.0 is possible if a high school student receives an A in an AP (Advanced Placement) class. There has been grade inflation in high school, but unlike in past generations, getting multiple As in AP classes are needed for admission to a top school. For example, your author's daughter had a 4.3 GPA but was 43rd in her class and was not accepted at UCLA, where her father graduated.

Native Americans were another ethnic group that helped build the skyscrapers of the early 20th century.

College-educated women have a negative birth rate (specifically 1.9 children per woman).

As rents in California are so high, the poverty rate is adjusted for the cost of living. Excluding the higher cost of rent and California's poverty is 13.4 percent, or just slightly higher than the national rate.

Borrowing five hundred billion dollars every year for ten years equates to trillion dollars every year or more money than all the COVID stimulus packages *combined*.

Not only is there is a shortage of land, but in the West, a chronic shortage of water. Water not just for residential use, but water for farming and commercial use.

In a state-managed pension program, just as is done with some lottery games, several states could join together.

In a test firing for Apollo 111 on the pad, "a small decision" to have a 100% oxygen environment created allowed for an electrical fire to spread very quickly, resulting in the deaths of three crewmembers.

APPENDIX

Imagine if America was a city of 100 households, and half the households were homeowners, and half were renters. Further, imagine each household has $10,000 in cash assets, and each homeowner has $10,000 in equity. The total wealth is 1.5 million dollars (50 renters times $10,000 and 50 homeowners times $20,000). In this scenario, homeowners own two-thirds of the total wealth.

Let's assume home prices (equity) increases by $10,000 per year, but as home prices have increased, fewer can afford to buy a home. Let's the percentage of renters increases by one percent every year. After ten years, the total wealth is five million dollars (sixty renters time $10,000, 40 homeowners times $10,000 in initial equity, plus 40 homeowners times ten years times $10,000 per year). In this scenario, after ten years, homeowners own eighty-three percent of all the wealth.

REFERENCES

Whenever possible, data cited in the text came from government sources, such as the Census Bureau and, in particular, the Bureau of Labor Statistics. Other data, like the number of longshoremen working on west coast ports came, came from a credible source, e.g., the longshoremen union's website.

Websites change. The links were active and correct when the final draft was being completed.

Preface

https://www.census.gov/data/tables/time-series/demo/income-poverty/historical-poverty-people.html

Chapter One: A brief history of capitalism and public assistance

https://www.academia.edu/4320866/Debtors_Prisons_in_America_An_Economic_Analysis
https://www.statista.com/statistics/183481/united-states-population-projection/
https://www.census.gov/library/publications/2019/demo
https://www.statista.com/statistics/1032399/wage-rank-american-civil-war-1861-1865
https://www.thomasnet.com/articles/top-suppliers/steel-suppliers-manufacturers
https://www.history.com/news/working-women-great-depression
https://www.nlm.nih.gov/hmd/diseases/early.html

https://www.history.com/news/civil-war-deadlier-than-previously-thought
https://www.essentialcivilwarcurriculum.com/civil-war-pensions.htm
www.history.com/topics/black-history/freedmens-bureau
www.slideshare.net/michellemoon67/history-of-orphanages
https://www.history.com/this-day-in-history/salvation-army-founded
https://www.ymca.net/history/founding.html
https://flocritco.org/
https://socialwelfare.library.vcu.edu/programs/child-welfarechild-labor/florence-crittenton-homes-history/
http://www.mfldymca.org/about_us/history_national.php
Proceedings of the National Conference of Charities and Correction at the Seventeenth Annual Session in Baltimore, Md., May 14-21, 1890. Pp.73-81
https://brewminate.com/the-poorhouse-americas-forgotten-institution/
https://www.macrotrends.net/1319/dow-jones-100-year-historical-chart
socialwelfare.library.vcu.edu/public-welfare/aid-to-dependent-children-the-legal-history/
https://socialwelfare.library.vcu.edu/eras/civil-war-reconstruction/charity-organization-societies-1877-1893/
https://aspe.hhs.gov/system/files/pdf/167036/1history.pdf
www.acf.hhs.gov/ofa/resource/caseload-data-afdc-1995-basic
www.history.com/topics/great-depression/civilian-conservation-corps
https://www.investopedia.com/ask/answers/who-or-what-is-dow-jones
www.horatioalgersociety.net/100_biography.html
https://www.aarp.org/money/low-income-assistance/info-10-2008/aresearch-import-772-FS20R.html
https://socialwelfare.library.vcu.edu/issues/poor-relief-almshouse/
https://socialwelfare.library.vcu.edu/programs/poor-relief-early-amer/
https://socialwelfare.library.vcu.edu/programs/child-welfarechild-labor/florence-crittenton-homes-history.
https://www.wkfamilylaw.com/child-support-debt-arrears.shtml

https://www.nytimes.com/1995/07/18/us/last-us-tv-maker-will-sell-control-to-koreans.html
https://www.census.gov/data/tables/time-series/demo/income-poverty/historical-poverty-people.html
https://www2.census.gov/prod2/decennial/documents/04187650ch1.pdf
https://flocritco.org/who-we-are/history/
https://www.careerexplorer.com/careers/radiologic-technologist/demographics/
onlineradiologytechnicianschools.com/how-long-does-it-take-to-become-a-radiology-tech/
https://phinational.org/wp-content/uploads/legacy/phi-home-care-workers-key-facts.pdf
www.cbpp.org/research/summary-of-final-tanf-rules
www.fas.org/sgp/crs/misc/R42627.pdf
https://www.thebalance.com/federal-poverty-level-definition-guidelines-chart-3305843
http://www.countyhealthrankings.org/take-action-to-improve-health/what-works-for-health/policies/full-child-support-pass-through-and-disregard
https://datausa.io/profile/soc/welding-soldering-brazing-workers
www.acf.hhs.gov/ofa/resource/major-provisions-of-the-welfare-law
www.acf.hhs.gov/ofa/resource/tanf-final-rule-executive-summary
https://www.irs.gov/pub/irs-prior/p954--2004.pdf

Chapter Two: The work ethic, faith, dads, and education

https://www.macworld.co.uk/feature/apple/history-of-apple-steve-jobs-mac-3606104/
https://www.britannica.com/topic/Apple-Inc
https://www.referenceforbusiness.com/biography/S-Z/Steward-David-L-1951.html

https://www.liveabout.com/childhood-biography-of-oprah-winfrey-2535832
https://www.notablebiographies.com/We-Z/Winfrey-Oprah.html
www.investopedia.com/articles/insights/072816/how-did-oprah-winfrey-get-rich.asp
https://www.cbo.gov/sites/default/files/114th-congress-2015-2016/reports/51495-youngmenreport.pdf
www.poverty.ucdavis.edu/faq/what-are-poverty-thresholds-today
https://work.chron.com/much-certified-nursing-assistant-paid-per-hour-8818.html
https://pubmed.ncbi.nlm.nih.gov/22458831/
https://fightthenewdrug.org/how-the-webcamming-industry-traps-the-financially-desperate/
www.ed.gov/about/overview/budget/index.html
https://www.philosophyforchildren.org/about/
http://blackboysreport.org/interactive-map-dashboard/
https://www.ibo.nyc.ny.us/iboreports/beyond-meal-status-a-new-measure-for-quantifying-poverty-levels-in-the-citys-schools-october-2015.html
https://ny.chalkbeat.org/2019/1/30/21108636/new-york-city-graduation-rate-ticks-up-to-76-percent-in-2018
https://www.npr.org/templates/story/story
https://news.gallup.com/poll/248837/church-membership-down-sharply-past-two-decades.aspx
https://www.cnbc.com/2015/01/21/porns-new-capitals-romania-and-colombia.html
www.bop.gov/about/statistics/statistics_inmate_race.jsp
https://www.borowitzclark.com/californias-wage-garnishment-rules-unpaid-taxes-child-support-consumer-deb
http://laschoolreport.com/californias-graduation-rate-rises-but-theres-no-improvement-in-getting-students-eligible-for-state-universities/
https://nces.ed.gov/fastfacts/display
www.charitynavigator.org/index

https://www.tandfonline.com/doi/abs
https://www.dancetheatreofharlem.org/our-history/
https://www.equityinhighered.org/indicators/secondary-school-completion/high-school-completion-rate-by-gender

Chapter 3: Food programs and Homeland Security

https://www.nytimes.com/2019/01/31/us/anchor-baby-birth-tourism.html
https://www.cbp.gov/newsroom/stats/sw-border-migration
https://www.americanbar.org/groups/law_aging/publications/bifocal/vol-40/volume-40-issue-6/older-immigrants/
https://ihldatabases.icrc.org/applic/ihl/ihl.nsf
https://naldc.nal.usda.gov/download/35895/PDF
https://livinghistoryfarm.org/farminginthe50s/money_09.html
www.cbpp.org/research/food-assistance/snap-helps-millions-of-children
https://frac.org/wp-content/uploads/cnnslp.pdf
www.cbpp.org/research/food-assistance/a-quick-guide-to-snap-eligibility-and-benefits
https://www.fns.usda.gov/pd/wic-program
https://data.worldbank.org/indicator/BX.TRF.PWKR.CD.DT?locations=MX
www.npr.org/sections/thesalt/2018/06/20/621391895/in-some-states-drug-felons-still-face-lifetime-ban-on-snap-benefits
www.aeaweb.org/research/charts/welfare-reform-food-stamps-recidivism
www.usda.gov/our-agency/about-usda/history/former-secretaries
www.aspe.hhs.gov/system/files/pdf/167036/7foodstamps.pdf
www.usafacts.org/reports/snap-food-stamps-assistance
https://www.ers.usda.gov/topics/food-nutrition-assistance/child-nutrition-programs/national-school-lunch-program
https://www.saferoutespartnership.org/sites/default/files/pdf/school_bus_cuts_national_stats_FINAL.pdf

http://www.act.org/content/dam/act/unsecured/documents/Info-Brief-2014-12.pdf
www.fns.usda.gov/wic/wic-eligibility-and-coverage-rates
https://fns-prod.azureedge.net/
https://www.fns.usda.gov/pd/wic-program
https://www.ers.usda.gov/topics/food-nutrition-assistance/wic-program/
www.wicworks.fns.usda.gov/wicworks/Learning Center/FP/powder_formula.pdf
www.fns-prod.azureedge.net/sites/default/files/pc96fr.pdf
www.nhlbi.nih.gov/health/educational/wecan/downloads/calreqtips.pdf
https://www.atu.org/work/school
https://www.cbpp.org/research/food-assistance/policy-basics-the-supplemental-nutrition-assistance-program-snap
https://www.beckershospitalreview.com/finance/10-hospital-bankruptcies-in-2018-091718.html
https://www.ers.usda.gov/topics/food-nutrition-assistance/wic-program/
https://www.fb.org/viewpoints/another-year-of-farm-labor-shortages
https://www.unco.edu/colorado-oral-history-migratory-labor-project/pdf/Bracero_Program_PowerPoint.pdf

Chapter 4: Public housing, crime, and homeownership

www.Georgiaencyclopedia.org/articles/arts-culture/techwood-homes
www.cbpp.org/research/housing/federal-rental-assistance-fact-sheets
www.huduser.gov/portal/sites/default/files/pdf/LengthofStay.pdf
https://www.hrw.org/report/2004/11/18/no-second-chance/people-criminal-records-denied-access-public-housing
https://nces.ed.gov/programs/digest/d16/tables/dt16_204.10.asp
https://www.urban.org/sites/default/files/publication/94146/trends-in-housing-problems-and-federal-housing-assistance.pdf
https://en.wikipedia.org/wiki/List_of_United_States_cities_by_crime_rate (citing FBI Statistics)

http://www.act.org/content/dam/act/unsecured/documents/Info-Brief-2014-12.pdf
https://nlihc.org/resource/public-housing-bans
https://nlihc.org/resource/hud-issues-final-rule-housing-protections-survivors-domestic-violence
https://www.aclu.org/sites/default/files/pdfs/subsidizedhousingdv.pdf
https://www.vera.org/publications/price-of-prisons-2015-state-spending-trends/price-of-prisons-2015-state-spending-trends/price-of-prisons-2015-state-spending-trends-prison-spending
https://fred.stlouisfed.org/series/HOWNRATEACS024510
https://ternercenter.berkeley.edu/blog/it-all-adds-up-the-cost-of-housing-development-fees-in-seven-california-cit
https://www.cnbc.com/id/100668336
https://www.irs.gov/pub/irs-prior/p954--2004.pdf
www.militarytimes.com/home-hq/2017/10/19/va-loan-history-lesson-the-program-in-the-1940s/
www.newsday.com/long-island/nassau/levittown-history-in-photos
www.bjs.gov/content/pub/pdf/ecp.pdf
www.federalreserve.gov/pubs/feds/2008/200859/200859pap.pdf
www.towncharts.com
nextstl.com/2013/01/understanding-st-louis-homicide-and-index-crimes-1943-2011/
www.habitat.org/multimedia/annual-report-2018/
detroitmi.gov/sites/detroitmi.localhost/files/2018-0
https://www.bjs.gov/content/pub/pdf/ecp.pdf
https://nces.ed.gov/pubs2016/2016040.pdf
https://nces.ed.gov/blogs/nces/2017/01/11/default
https://www.prisonpolicy.org/blog/2016/04/01/literacy/
www.justice.gov/jmd/page/file/1033161/download
http://dynamic.stlouis-mo.gov/census/city.cfm
https://www.bestplaces.net/economy/city/arizona/scottsdale
https://www.bestplaces.net/economy/city/california/irvine
www.history.com/topics/world-war-ii/gi-bill
www.latimes.com/archives/la-xpm-1988-06-21-fi-4744-story.html

https://www.aplu.org/projects-and-initiatives/college-costs-tuition-and-financial-aid/publicuvalues/student-debt.html

Chapter Five: Poverty, parenting, and child care

https://eclkc.ohs.acf.hhs.gov/policy/pi/acf-pi-hs-20-02
https://eclkc.ohs.acf.hhs.gov/about-us/article/head-start-program-facts-fiscal-year-2019
https://turbotax.intuit.com/tax-tips/family/deducting-summer-camps-and-daycare-with-the-child-and-dependent-care-credit
https://www.acf.hhs.gov/occ/news/decreasing-number-family-child-care-providers-united-states
www.sciencedirect.com/science/article/pii/S0190740916303139
https://www.nps.gov/subjects/infrastructure/deferred-maintenance.htm

Chapter Six: The apex and base of the pyramid

https://www.epi.org/publication/ceo-compensation-2018/
https://www.marketwatch.com/story/fortune-500-ceos-are-paid-from-double-to-5000-times-more-than-their-employees-2018-05-16
https://www.inc.com/barbara-weltman/executive-compensation-deduction-tax-guide.html
https://www.brookings.edu/blog/up-front/2019/06/25/six-facts-about-wealth-in-the-united-states/
https://www.taxpolicycenter.org/statistics/historical-capital-gains-and-taxes
https://www.advfn.com/nyse/newyorkstockexchange.asp
www.en.wikipedia.org/wiki/Luxurytax
https://dqydj.com/how-many-millionaires-decamillionaires-america/
https://aflcio.org/paywatch/highest-paid-ceos
https://work.chron.com/much-money-nfl-player-make-year-2377.html
https://www.usatoday.com/sports/mlb/salaries/2019/team/all/
https://www.boxofficemojo.com/year/

https://archive.thinkprogress.org/average-japanese-ceo-earns-one-sixth-as-much-as-american-ceos

https://www.cato.org/publications/tax-budget-bulletin/earned-income-tax-credit-small-benefits-large-costs

https://stats.oecd.org/Index.asp

https://www.irs.gov/credits-deductions/individuals/earned-income-tax-credit/earned-income-tax-credit-income-limits-and-maximum-credit-amounts

https://www.debt.org/medical/medicaid-costs/https://www.kff.org/other/state-indicator/distribution-byhttps://www.theatlantic.com/education/archive/2019/02/the-explosion-of-women-teachers

https://www.taxpolicycenter.org/sites/default/files/publication/157276/expanding_the_eitc_0.pdf

https://www.cnbc.com/2019/02/21/here-are-5-ways-the-super-rich-manage-to-pay-lower-taxes.html

https://www.npr.org/2019/09/10/759512938/u-s-census-bureau-reports-poverty-rate-down-but-millions-still-poor

https://www.kff.org/other/state-indicator/distribution-by-fpl

https://cepr.net/documents/publications/fast-food-workers-2013-08.pdf

https://www.samhsa.gov/sites/default/files/programs_campaigns/homelessness_programs_resources/

https://bench.co/blog/operations/unemployment-benefits-by-state/ -fact sheet-current-statistics-prevalence-characteristics-homelessness.pdf

https://www.statista.com/statistics/241530/birth-rate-by-family-income-in-the-us/

https://www.statista.com/statistics/245409/change-in-total-medicaid-spending-and-enrollment-since-1998/

https://www.cms.gov/Research-Statistics-Data-and-Systems/Statistics-Trends-and-Reports/NationalHealthExpendData

https://www.nsf.gov/about/budget/fy2021/index.jsp

https://dmdatabases.com/databases/business-mailing-lists/how-many-businesses

Chapter 7: The changing workforce and child support

https://www.payscale.com/research/US/Job=Longshoreman
https://unctad.org/en/PublicationsLibrary/dtl2018d1_en.pdf
https://www.unionfacts.com/union/Longshore
https://www.cdc.gov/niosh/mining/userfiles/works/pdfs/2012-152.pdf
https://www.miningreview.com/top-stories/infographic-women-in-the-mining-industry-what-the-stats-say/
https://en.wikipedia.org/wiki/Coal_mining_in_the_United_States#/media/File:US_Coal_Mining_Employment_1890-2014.png
https://www.seia.org/solar-industry-research-data
https://www.theatlantic.com/education/archive/2019/02/the-explosion-of-women-teachers/582622/
https://www.ncbi.nlm.nih.gov/pmc/articles/PMC314508/
https://www.gov.ca.gov/2020/03/02/governor-newsom-releases-2019-judicial-appointment-data
https://datausa.io/profile/soc/counselors
https://www.bls.gov/oes/2017/may/oes435081.htm
https://constructioncoverage.com/research/cities-with-the-most-women-in-construction-2020
https://www.jurist.org/commentary/2019/03/pisarcik-women-outnumber-men-in-law-school/
https://www.diversityinc.com/more-black-men-lawyers-but-racial-gap-remains/
https://www.apa.org/workforce/publications/13-demographic.
https://www.nbcnews.com/health/health-news/why-dearth-black-men-medicine-worrisome-n885851
http://www.jbhe.com/news_views/65_gendergap.html.
https://www.athenahealth.com/knowledge-hub/practice-management/healthcare-future-female
https://www.hci.edu/hci-news-blog/730-male-nursing-statistics
https://news.cornell.edu/stories/2007/06/why-women-become-veterinarians-not-engineers
https://nces.ed.gov/fastfacts/display.asp

https://work.chron.com/union-pay-journeyman-grocery-clerk-28112.html
https://nces.ed.gov/programs/coe
https://newsroom.courts.ca.gov/news/survey-california-bench-growing-more-diverse
https://blog.oup.com/2011/06/librarian-census
https://www.bls.gov/oes/current/oes432021.htm
https://www.bls.gov/cps/cpsaat11.htm
https://www.census.gov/newsroom/blogs/random-samplings/2017/10/women-manufacturing.html
https://www.motorbiscuit.com/american-cars-that-are-barely-made-in-america/
https://www.bls.gov
https://www.pewresearch.org/
https://www.bls.gov/ooh/sales/cashiers.htm
https://datausa.io/profile/soc/cashiers#
https://www.bls.gov/ooh/transportation-and-material-moving/delivery-truck-drivers-and-driver-sales-workers.htm#tab-6
https://www.businessinsider.com/pretty-waitresses-earn-bigger-tips-from-women-2015-9
https://www.statista.com/statistics/818602/online-and-offline-grocery-market-share-of-leading-grocery-retailers-us/
https://www.ift.org/news-and-publications/food-technology-magazine/issues/2020/january
https://www.statista.com/statistics/193533/growth-of-global-air-traffic-passenger-demand/
https://atpflightschool.com/become-a-pilot
https://www.reuters.com/article/us-japan-ageing-robots-widerimage/aging-japan-robots-may-have-role-in-future-of-elder-care-id
https://www.statista.com/statistics/693807/uber-employee-gender-global/
https://www.eater.com/2021/4/13/22381880/dominos-tests-self-driving-delivery-vehicle-in-houston

https://www.insurancejournal.com/news/national/2018/08/30/499668.htm
https://www.statista.com/statistics/788109/amazon-retail-market-share-usa/
https://www.ncsl.org/research/human-services/welfare-reform-family-cap-policies.aspx
https://www.businessinsider.com/how-much-does-it-cost-to-have-a-baby-2018-4
https://bigthink.com/mind-brain/adult-brain
https://www.sagepub.com/sites/default/files/upm-binaries/60294_Chapter_23.pdf
https://www.bls.gov/ooh/transportation-and-material-moving/railroad-occupations.htm
https://education.costhelper.com/aircraft-mechanic-school.html
https://datausa.io/profile/soc/phlebotomists#
https://www.careerexplorer.com/careers
https://www.aoa.org/news/inside-optometry/the-future-is-female
https://www.bls.gov/cps
https://www.statista.com/statistics/653789/average-age-of-tech-company-employees/
https://www.statista.com/statistics/242729/number-of-employees-in-the-us-apparel-manufacturing-industry/
https://www.zippia.com/cable-installer-jobs/demographics
https://www.mswmanagement.com/collection/article/13024952/women-in-waste.
https://bigtruckrental.com/side-loader-garbage-truck-rental-service/side-loader-history/
http://www.policyfuse.com/2017/03/automation-does-not-always-mean-that.html
https://www.bls.gov/ooh/office-and-administrative-support/tellers.htm#tab-6
https://www.census.gov/popclock/

Chapter Eight: The three-legged stool meets the 21St Century

https://www.ssa.gov/news/press/factsheets/basicfact-alt.pdf
https://www.cbpp.org/research/social-security/what-the-2020-trustees-report-shows-about-social-security
https://money.usnews.com/money/retirement/social-security/articles
https://data.oecd.org/pop/working-age-population.htm
https://www.ici.org/faqs/faq/401k/
https://www.kff.org/medicare/issue-brief/how-many-seniors-live-in-poverty
https://www.bankrate.com/retirement/average-monthly-social-security-check/
www.ssa.gov
www.census.gov/newsroom/blogs/random-samplings/2017/09/outlying_older_ameri.html
https://www.valuepenguin.com/banking/average-savings-account-balance:
https://www.pbgc.gov/about/who-we-are/pg/history-of-pbgc
https://www.bls.gov/opub/mlr/1991/12/art3full.pdf
https://www.payingforseniorcare.com/federal-poverty-level
https://www.treasurer.ca.gov/calsavers/meeting/2020/20200415/staff/2.2.pdf
https://www.cnbc.com/2019/07/01/california-is-the-latest-state-to-help-millions-join-retirement-plans.html
https://www.ncbi.nlm.nih.gov/pmc/articles
https://www.cdc.gov/tobacco/disparities/low-ses/index.htm
https://www.tobaccofreekids.org/assets/factsheets/0097.pdf
https://www.verywellhealth.com/what-is-the-average-age-for-lung-cancer-2249260
https://www.tobaccofreekids.org/assets/factsheets/0275.pdf
https://www.ncbi.nlm.nih.gov/pmc/articles

https://www.accc-cancer.org/docs/projects/resources/pdf/occm-environmental-scan-highlights-for-lung-cancer-patients-on-medicaid
https://taxfoundation.org/2019-state-cigarette-tax-rankings/
https://www.statista.com/statistics/248964/revenues-from-tobacco-tax-and-forecast-in-the-us
https://www.ncbi.nlm.nih.gov/pmc/articles/PMC1361028/
https://euthanasia.procon.org/state-by-state-physician-assisted-suicide-statistics/
https://www.nimh.nih.gov/health/statistics/suicide.shtml
https://pubmed.ncbi.nlm.nih.gov/26562758/
https://www.ajmc.com/view/influenza-in-older-patients-a-call-to-action-and-recent-updates-for-vaccinations
https://www.ncbi.nlm.nih.gov/pmc/articles
https://medicarenursingservices.com/index.php/en/mediblog/item/19-why-are-men-reluctant-medical-help

Chapter 9: The American Dream and social services

https://transportgeography.org/
https://www.passblue.com/2017/10/02/when-deaths-exceed-births-in-countries-and-the-immigration-effect/
https://fred.stlouisfed.org/series/MSPUS
https://www.forbes.com/sites/mikepatton/2016/02/29/u-s-role-in-global-economy-declines-nearly-50
https://www.statista.com/statistics/270267/united-states-share-of-global-gross-domestic-product-gdp/
https://www.bbc.com/news/world-asia-china-46772503
https://www.weforum.org/agenda/2020/07/largest-global-economies-1992-2008-2024
http://www.laalmanac.com/population/po02.php
www.census.gov/prod/1/pop/profile/95/p23-189.pdf
https://www.census.gov/quickfacts

https://www.npr.org/2019/02/13/694199256/u-s-national-debt-hits-22-trillion-a-new-record-thats-predicted-to-fall

https://www.pewresearch.org/fact-tank/2019/07/24/facts-about-the-national-debt

https://fred.stlouisfed.org/series/ATNHPIUS11260Q

https://www.lendingtree.com/home/mortgage/single-women-own-more-homes-than-single-men-do/

https://dqydj.com/historical-home-prices/

https://dqydj.com/household-income-by-year/

https://www.census.gov/housing/hvs/data/charts/fig08.pdf

https://www.lendingtree.com/home/mortgage/homeownership-gender-gap-study

https://www.brookings.edu/blog/the-avenue/2019/01/15/three-things-that-matter-for-upward-mobility-in-the-labor-market/

https://www.statista.com/statistics/183481/united-states-population-projection/

Made in United States
Orlando, FL
27 April 2022